Skillbuilding Mastery

By
Barbara Grace Ellsworth
Mesa Community College
Mesa, Arizona

Skillbuilding Mastery

by
Barbara G. Ellsworth
Mesa Community College
Mesa, Arizona

Copyright © 1993-2016
By ELLSWORTH PUBLISHING COMPANY
Chandler, AZ

For Information, please contact:

Ellsworth Publishing Company
P.O. Box 6727
Chandler, AZ 85246
www.EllsworthPublishing.com

PRINTED IN THE UNITED STATES OF AMERICA

Important Information About The Course:

★ **Cutting Edge Web-based keyboarding features:**
  - Courses for elementary, middle school, high school, and college.
  - No software to install, update, maintain. All your school needs to maintain is an Internet connection. Upgrades are completed by EPC and available immediately, and are FREE.
  - Courses are self paced; students can work from anywhere (e.g. classroom, home, library, etc).
  - NO PAPERS TO GRADE, HANDLE, PRINT, OR TURN IN TO INSTRUCTOR due to an outstanding teacher management system.
  - Mid-Term and Final Grades are automatically calculated.
  - Monitor and manage all student data online. View scores and grades from the Internet.
  - Special unique software feature prevents students from taking their eyes off the textbook. Solves the age-old problem of students watching their hands or the screen.
  - Use Schedule Manager to select start/end dates, and days/times that students are allowed to work. (Example: If a student is found to be having a friend outside of class do some of his/her work, you can schedule that student's data file only to open during class time).
  - Internal Messaging system to send messages of encouragement/praise to students and receive student replies.
  - Software can be individualized to advanced or special needs students if desired.
  - Create your own custom lessons (create your own 'course within a course').
  - *Nuts 'n' Bolts of Formatting* downloadable textbook free to users of EPC courses—covering Basic Word Concepts, Fax Applications, Interoffice Memos, Business Letters, Proofreader's Marks, Tables, Business Reports, Itineraries, Agendas-Minutes-News Releases, Outlines, Creating Flyers, and Job Search Skills. Directions are on the left and pictures and illustrations on the right—very visual. *We keep up with the latest software versions; schools don't have to purchase thick textbooks that include formatting which become obsolete with each software update.*
  - *Introduction to Microsoft Applications is* downloadable textbook free to users of EPC courses (latest versions)—covering Publisher, Excel, Access, and PowerPoint. Directions are on the left and pictures and illustrations on the right—very visual.
  - Free Site License option to colleges.

★ **There are six essential keyboarding techniques that students should master:**
  - The first day of class students should view the audio/video presentation that illustrates the six essential keyboarding techniques (S. E. C. R. E. T) that are basic to acquiring good keyboarding skills. The keyboarding course demo covers everything necessary for students to begin immediately. Demo's are found on the web site www.KeyboardingOnline.com.

★ **Typists learn speed and accuracy from Lesson 1:**
  - The course standards are created in the Setup by the teacher in the Teacher Manager. Set the Grading Scale for the speed students should achieve by the end of the semester/term. Practice each timing, from Lesson 1, until that speed is reached. If the timing meets the accuracy rate in the Setup, it will record to the Progress Report, from which grades are calculated. Lesson 1 is very easy to assist students in achieving the speed/accuracy goals. This is Competency Based Instruction—master each practice timing until the speed/accuracy goal is achieved before continuing to the next practice timing. All lessons begin with 15– and 30-second timings to encourage the fingers to move quickly.

Appendix

Quite often you will use your keyboarding skills to prepare letters, memos, and other business type documents. There are a multitude of word processing programs available and instructions will vary depending upon the word processing program chosen.

Some popular word processing programs you may find:

Microsoft Word

Libre Office (from www.LibreOffice.org a FREE full-featured office productivity suite that will even read and save MS Office formats.) We certainly recommend this suite for budget minded users.

Ellsworth Publishing Co. (EPC) offers a free textbook in PDF format that addresses many document formatting concepts. This text is titled *"Nuts and Bolts of Formatting"*, and is available as a free download for current users of EPC products. For our Internet users, this PDF book will be listed at the bottom of the screen showing the licensed products for your school.

★ **Experienced typists can improve 10-20 wpm faster than the current speed:**
   - Experienced typists can take the 5-minute *Course Entry* timing, raise the grading scale by 10-20 wpm, and practice each timing until the new goal is reached.

★ **Block the timing screen to encourage students to keep their eyes on the copy, not their fingers or the keys:**
   - Fast and productive typists can type without looking at their keys.
   - The timing screen can be blocked so students cannot see what they have typed until after the practice timing. If they look away from the copy to their fingers or keys, they will usually lose their place and make an error. All lessons begin with 15-second timings and usually 0 errors (set by instructor). If the errors allowed are exceeded the timing score will not record. Students learn from the beginning to keep their eyes on the copy, which helps them learn the keys faster.

★ **Set a timer timeout:**
   - This setting allows you to encourage students to continue typing until the timer finishes. If they stop early, their lesson will reset and they will receive no score.
   - This feature is especially helpful, when combined with the 'Block Timing Screen', for breaking bad habits like Hunting and Pecking. Virtually 100% effective!

★ **Alphabetic, Punctuation, Number, and Symbol keys are reviewed**
   - Section A in the textbook contains information necessary to enable students to get started quickly and progress independently on their own. **It should be read by teachers and students.** Section B review all keyboard letters:
      - Section B is designed to build speed and accuracy while reviewing the keys A-Z.
      - Timings range from 15 second to 5 minute, with more emphasis on longer timings.
      - 5 Proofreading lessons.

★ **Create your own custom lessons:**
   - Instructors can create their own timed and graded lessons. These created lessons become part of the student's progress report and grade (created lessons are treated just like any other lesson in the course).
   - This allows instructors to create their own 'course within a course'. Do students need extra practice with medical terminologies, longer timings, etc.? Create your own lessons to fit your own needs!

Time Requirements:
   - Approximately 50-60 hours to complete all lessons.
   - Prerequisite skill of 35 WPM.

Supporting Materials:
No additional materials are necessary for either the teacher or student—the courses are self-contained with the textbook and software only.

5-Minute Timing — Who Was the Father of Our Constitution

James Madison was about five feet six inches tall and weighed only about one hundred pounds. As a child he was sickly, and as a young man he was skinny and frail. He went to Princeton University and graduated in two years instead of four. He was not a sociable person and never participated in sports. He just did not distinguish himself in any way. Eleven of the twelve graduates participated in the graduation program. Madison's only participation was to receive his diploma. He was shy with women. When he finally became engaged, the girl broke the engagement after only six weeks. With a record like this, you would have thought that James Madison would never amount to anything. At the age of thirty-six, he became one of the representatives of Virginia at the Constitutional Convention in Philadelphia. Nobody came better prepared intellectually than he. Ten years earlier he had drafted the Virginia Plan of Union, and had read and analyzed hundreds of books on history, political theory, and workings of government. After four months, the Constitution was drafted, and one of the most important contributors was James Madison. He overcame opposition to the ratification of the Constitution in Virginia, and his brilliant Federalist Papers were instrumental in winning quick support from the rest of the country. He was a man of intelligence, knowledge, and hard work. His contributions to our country earned James Madison the title of Father of the Constitution.

About the Author:

Barbara G. Ellsworth has taught at Mesa Community College for 45+ years (she says she started teaching when she was 12). For many years Mrs. Ellsworth taught Business Machines. During that time she wrote and published over 42 workbooks for various Ten-Key and calculating machines. Mrs. Ellsworth currently has written and published five web-based courses—*Ten Key Mastery, Keyboard Mastery, Keyboard Short Course, Skillbuilding Mastery, Keyboarding For Kids (Grades 1-6), Nuts 'n' Bolts Formatting, and Introduction to MS Applications.* Her products are found at all educational levels—K-12, College/Adult, job corps., as well as in government institutions and commercial businesses.

Tutorials, demonstrations, course descriptions, downloads, current syllabi, and online course information can be seen at:

www.EllsworthPublishing.com

Course Descriptions

★ **TEN KEY MASTERY** — (Approximately 30 hours) To teach the numeric keypad with speed and accuracy. Course includes three actual employment tests for students to practice. To achieve employment standards, it is recommended to be a quarter or semester course.

★ **KEYBOARD MASTERY** — (Approximately 50-60 hours) To teach the alpha/numeric keyboard to beginners and to those who haven't typed in a long time and have rusty skills. The course contains 15-second to 5-minute timings that cover the basics. This course can be customized for either a semester or a quarter course.

★ **KEYBOARD SHORT COURSE** — (Approximately 25 hours) A shortened version of KEYBOARD MASTERY. It covers the alphabetic and punctuation keys (no numeric or symbol keys). It is designed for approximately 5 - 9 weeks. The course contains mainly 15-second timings which push for speed and accuracy, and includes 30-second, 1- and 2-minute timings. This course is excellent for beginners and experienced typists who need to raise their skills quickly.

★ **SKILLBUILDING MASTERY** — (Approximately 50-60 hours) Advanced Keyboarding. Covers alpha and numeric/symbol keys with 15-second to 5-minute timings designed to bring students to employable levels of speed and accuracy. It is recommended that students type approximately 32-35 wpm before taking this course.

★ **KEYBOARDING FOR KIDS** — (Approximately 20-40 hours) For Grades 1 - 6. Teaches keyboarding correctly to children at a time when they are exposed to computers, and to prevent the formation of bad keyboarding habits. The short timings and textbook help keep student's eyes away from the screen and fingers. Students are rewarded with graphics of praise when they meet their goal.

★ **NUTS 'n' BOLTS FORMATTING** — A FREE download (PDF book) for current EPC users covering basic document processing—letters, tables, faxes, memos, business reports, etc.

★ **INTRODUCTION TO MICROSOFT APPLICATIONS** — A FREE download (PDF book) for current EPC users covering: Windows, Publisher, Excel, Access, and PowerPoint.

5-Minute Timing — More Tips on Being an Effective Speaker

If you are called upon to give a speech, there are some tricks of the trade that will help your audience feel involved in your presentation. First, as soon as possible use a personal example to establish some kind of direct relationship with the group you are addressing. If you are speaking to a political group, tell the audience how you first became active in politics. Another way to open the lines of communication is to use the names of people in the audience. One famous speaker always asked the master of ceremonies during luncheons who certain people were. When he arose to speak, it became evident why he asked people's names. He cleverly wove some of the names he had learned into his talk. You could see the evident pleasure on the faces of the people in the audience and could sense their friendliness towards the speaker. Another speaking technique is to involve your audience as a partner in your speeches. Get them involved in your speech. You might want to choose some member of the audience to help you demonstrate a point or dramatize an idea. Asking questions and calling on people for responses is very effective. It could be something as simple as answering a yes or no question by raising their hands. One particular speaker always had her audience repeat an important point during her speech. Speakers who follow these principles are using audience participation to achieve active listening. The audience will remember these speakers.

Why should I learn keyboarding?

The most simple answer is a one word answer: **Productivity**.

The future workforce you will be a part of, and compete with, is increasingly global. This means that you will be competing with other persons not in your city, or even in your state. Companies and their workforce must compete with workers in other countries willing to do the same job, and often times for less money. How do U.S. companies compete against lower wage countries and a workforce eager for employment? Getting more work done with fewer hours worked = Productivity.

In the 21st century, a common theme of distress is the outsourcing of jobs outside of the U.S. Consider the following statement from the May 2004 issue of Business 2.0 (full PDF of article available at: www.KeyboardingOnline.com/Articles/Keyboarding_And_Outsourcing.pdf)

*"For American service workers to hang on to their jobs, they will have to make similar changes. Barry P. Bosworth, a senior fellow in economic studies at the Brookings Institution, points out that the fastest-growing service fields are the engineering and management of computerized sales and supply systems. To shine in those careers, he says, **workers have to master at least four skills: computer literacy, <u>typing</u>, an understanding of how complex organizations work, and the ability to deal with people (either in person or electronically). Yet despite the fact that services account for 80 percent of private-sector employment, how many high schools require courses in <u>typing</u>, computer science, operations research, and interpersonal relations?** Talk about productivity: If critics want to be truly effective at keeping jobs at home, they should stop scolding businesses and start crusading for better education reform."*

<u>But Voice Recognition software is going to replace the keyboard, right</u>? For debate, we will look at the best case scenario for Voice/Speech recognition software and we will assume that recognition software has matured into the perfect product and has overcome the following hurdles:

(1) No problems recognizing accents, slurred speech, speech when you are sick, speech from different parts of the country, or sounds that people sometimes misarticulate (just ask a Speech-Language pathologist).
(2) It needs no training, it instantly recognizes the speech characteristics of any person that sits down at any given computer.
(3) The software is found everywhere and on every computer.
(4) The software has mastered short-cuts and enhancements that make speaking faster in all ways rather than typing/keyboarding (think web browsing and data entry).

Assuming that recognition software is perfect, there are many social and economic issues that will always necessitate keyboarding skills. If you can answer 'Yes' to the following situations, then the keyboard will become obsolete, otherwise, better plan on keeping it as part of your curriculum:

(1) In your lab, it would be preferable to have students dictate their term papers/book reports to the computer. The noise would not be a distraction.
(2) During class (K-12 or college classes), it would be best if students could dictate lecture notes into their laptop rather than have to type them.
(3) While attending a conference, you decide to use one of the email stations. You would rather dictate your email alongside everyone else who is dictating their emails (privacy, privacy, privacy).
(4) In an office environment, all secretaries and data-entry employees could dictate memos, reports, etc., without disturbing employees or worrying about confidentiality.
(5) and so on, and so on.

There are social and privacy reasons that can never be overcome with even the best recognition software. There will certainly be uses for voice recognition software, but it will not make the keyboard obsolete.

5-Minute Timing — The Most Valuable Personality Traits of a Good Manager

Many, many years ago managers didn't waste much time on diplomacy or trying to motivate people. They just gave the orders and employees carried them out. If they didn't, they lost their job. Times have changed today. The emphasis now is on good human relations, on treating employees in a way that encourages them to want to perform well for you. It makes for a much better working environment and, in most cases, works a lot better than a dictatorial environment. No matter how much you know about management techniques, it's an obvious fact that people will respond better to your leadership if they like you. The ability to make people like you is one of the most valuable personality traits you can possibly develop. It will enhance all your other abilities. It is a mark of a good leader.

So, what makes people like you? Good humor, kindness, appreciation of their interests and feelings, keeping confidences, and fair treatment will make other people like you. Learn to be humble in the presence of others. Develop enough self-confidence to be able to laugh at yourself once in awhile. On the other hand, snobbishness toward those in lesser authority is sure to cause sizzling resentments. Watch out for rudeness. It has been said that rudeness is a little person's attempt to exert control. It is a cheap imitation of power.

Table of Contents:

COURSE DESCRIPTION

SECTION A—GENERAL INFORMATION   A-1

SECTION B—SkillBuilding   B-1

5-Minute Timing — Tips on Being an Effective Speaker

Would you like a tip on being an effective speaker? Make your speech interesting by relating the main idea to a personal experience. Many speakers make speeches about subjects like Patriotism, or Democracy, or Justice, and frantically search through a book of quotations or a speaker's handbook for all occasions. They might throw together some generalizations vaguely remembered from a political science course they once took in college. The result is just what you would expect. We are all dying to hear such speeches. Now, there may be times you may be called upon to give a speech on just such subjects. However, you can always make it interesting by relating the concepts to personal experiences in your own life or the lives of others. Stories illustrating your points are what will be remembered. If your speech is on democracy and freedom, perhaps you could recall the time you met that interesting couple from communist China in the J. C. Penney's store. Relate some of the reasons why they said they fled their homeland and do not want to return. What about that friend that escaped from East Berlin when the wall was there? These are the stories that will not only illustrate the main idea of your speech but they will be remembered by an audience. Speeches that have personal experiences to emphasize its important points will have the audience sitting on the edge of their seats.

Table of Contents continued:

SECTION B—SkillBuilding continued

5-Minute Timing — How to Handle Mistakes

People who stand still may avoid stubbing their toes, but they won't make much progress. Every company and every department needs supervisors with the courage to try new ideas and run the risk of making mistakes. Progress doesn't come any other way. Peter Drucker, a well-known management consultant, says that the better the worker, the more mistakes he will make and the more new things he will experiment with. He says he would never promote a person, man or woman, into a top-level job who never made mistakes. No one likes to make a mistake. All managers and supervisors worth their salt would rather avoid errors. However, who can tell for sure whether a new idea will work or not until it actually has been tried? If the possible gains are far more than the potential loss, it is worth trying. Good managers are quite cautious, but not too cautious. If an excessive fear of mistakes is shown, their associates pick up on that and initiative and zeal can easily be stifled. People get super cautious if every little mistake tends to get them into a jam. If someone slips up, assess the situation and decide what corrective action to take. Do you place the emphasis, not on the mistake, but on seeing that your people understand why something didn't work so they don't make the same mistake twice? It is great to strive for failure-proof performance, but not at the expense of progress.

SECTION A

General Information

5-Minute Timing — The High Cost of Getting Even

The cost of getting even is very high. When we hate our enemies, we are giving them power over us: power over our sleep, our appetites, our blood pressure, our health, and our happiness. Our enemies would dance with joy if only they knew how they were worrying us. Our hate is not hurting them at all, but it is turning our own days into hellish turmoil. If selfish people try to take advantage of you, cross them off your list, but don't try to get even. When you try to get even, you hurt yourself more than you hurt the other person. If someone habitually offends you, consider the source. It has been said that rudeness is the attempt of a weak and inadequate person to exercise control. Wouldn't our enemies rub their hands with glee if they knew that our hate for them was exhausting us, making us tired and nervous, ruining our looks, giving us heart trouble, and probably shortening our lives? If we can't love our enemies, let's at least love ourselves enough that we won't permit our enemies to seize control of our happiness, our health, and our looks. Shakespeare summed it all up by writing: Heat not a furnace for your foe so hot, that it do singe yourself. We may not be saintly enough to love our enemies, but for the sake of our health and happiness let's at least forgive them and forget them. Confucious once said: "To be wronged or robbed is nothing unless you continue to remember it."

KNOW YOUR PROGRAM — Watch the course demo at www.KeyboardingOnline.com

1. To become an excellent typist there are <u>six absolutely essential techniques</u>:

   S _ _ **U** _ Straight, a _ _ _ and w _ _ _ _ _ straight.

   E _ _ _ on the b _ _ _ .

   C _ _ _ _ _ _ _ **F** _ _ _ _ _ _ _ _ _. Keep your " _ " finger on the " _ " key when depressing the Enter key. Keep your fingers near the H _ _ _ R _ _ . Each finger depresses its own keys.

   R _ _ _ _ _ _ _ _ _ **R** _ _ _ _ _ . Keep an even, steady pace. Eliminate pauses.

   E _ _ _ _ _ _ _ _ errors properly, if allowed by your teacher.

   T _ _ **K** _ _ _ as if they were hot.

2. If your typing area turns grey and cannot see what you have typed your instructor has enabled the B_ _ _ _out Timing is enabled.

3. The U _ _ _ I _ _ _ screen is where you can change your password.

4. The S _ _ _ _ contains all of your course standards. Click on the tabs to see the course standards.

5. The E _ _ _ _ _ A _ _ _ _ _ _ column shows the accuracy needed to have a timing recorded. If you have too many errors, take the timing again.

6. When you finish a lesson, a c _ _ _ _ _ m _ _ _ will appear in the box on the left.

7. On single line exercises do not press the S _ _ _ _ _ _ _ at the end of the line, press the E _ _ _ _ key and keep going until the timer stops. The timer begins when the first key is depressed.

8. If you begin a timing with errors you can start over by clicking on the T _ _ _ _ button.

9. To make letters larger on the screen move the A _ _ _ _ _ F _ _ _ button to the right.

10. The P _ _ _ _ _ _ _ R _ _ _ _ _ shows your best timing scores.

11. The current grade and final grade are based on the B _ _ _ score for each lesson line on the Progress Report.

12. The C _ _ _ _ _ _ Grade Report shows your overall average WPM (non-weighted) with a grading scale to help you evaluate your progress.

13. The F _ _ _ _ Grade Report shows your final weighted timing grade when A _ _ the assigned lessons have been completed.

14. Can you go back to your Progress Report at any time and practice to improve your scores and grade? (Yes / No)

15. The M _ _ _ _ _ _ Center can be used to communicate with your instructor.

5-Minute Timing — A Good Leader Is Not a Log

One of Aesop's fables was about frogs that wanted a leader. Over and over again they kept asking the god, Zeus, to send them one. Zeus finally answered by placing a log into their pond. This was to be their leader. For a time the frogs were happy. Soon they found that they could jump all over their new leader and it offered no resistance. It just floated around without purpose or direction. This soon exasperated the frogs. They decided they wanted a strong leader. The frogs went back to Zeus and complained about the lack of direction from their new leader. This time Zeus gave them a stork. The stork looked stately like a leader should. He stood tall and walked with dignity. The frogs were delighted as the great bird strode about the pond. The stork didn't really communicate with the frogs, but it did impress them when it made a clatter with its bill and especially when it ascended in flight and soared overhead.

One day the stork began eating the frogs and panic set in. Only then did the frogs realize that leadership was more than looks and charisma. A quality leader, they learned, had to have more purpose and direction than a log, but be less self-serving than a stork. A good leader had to be loyal and sensitive to the needs of the frogs in the pond.

Getting Started

<u>**Keyboarding Online:**</u>

1. Open your Internet browser (i.e. Internet Explorer, Firefox, Chrome, Safari, etc.)
2. Go to: login.KeyboardingOnline.com.
3. The school login and password is given by your instructor (EPC does not provide login instructions to students, this must be provided by your instructor). Your instructor may have qualification or attendance requirements needed before beginning the online class.
4. Click on the icon for your course.
5. (A) Choose your class, (B) Select your name.
6. Enter your ID/Password, this is different from the login/password used to get into login.KeyboardingOnline.com (your instructor will inform you of your ID/Password). You are now into your course.
7. Click the *Setup* in the main menu to see the course standards. Click on *Introduction* and go through all steps. Click *Lessons Menu* to take timings.
8. You will be prompted for an access code when opening any lesson screen. If you do not have an online access code on the easel of this book, you may purchase a code at: store.KeyboardingOnline.com.

15.   Late in the fifteenth century, two young and
zealous wood-carving apprentices in France confided in
each other their craving to study painting. Such study
would take money and both Hans and Albrecht had none.
Their joint solution was to have one work and earn
money while the other one studied. When the lucky one
became rich and famous, he would work and aid the other
one. They tossed a coin and Albrecht won. Albrecht
quickly went to Venice to study painting while Hans
worked as a blacksmith. After many hard years, at last
Albrecht returned home as an independent master. Now it
was his turn to help Hans. However, when Albrecht
looked at his friend, tears welled in his eyes. Only
then did he discover the extent of his friend's
sacrifice. The years of heavy labor in the blacksmith
shop had calloused and enlarged Hans' sensitive hands.
Hans could never be a painter. In humble gratitude to
Hans for his years of sacrifice, the great artist,
Albrecht Durer, painted a portrait of the work-worn
hands that sacrificed so much so that he might develop
his talent. He presented this painting of praying hands
to his devoted friend. Today, this masterpiece is a
symbol of love and sacrifice and is familiar to
millions of people throughout the world.

SETUP—ENTERING COURSE STANDARDS

The *Setup* screens ask for *Name*, *ID#*, *Options*, *Timing Weights*, *Sections*, and *Grading Scale*. These course standards will appear on the *Final Grade Report*. (For the Internet version, the instructor would already have completed the *Setup* for you).

Name: First and last name.

ID#:   Roster number/student ID# Students will need to know this number/word in order to open their file (files are password protected).

Options: *Errors Allowed*—timings meeting the errors allowed will save (top three scores meeting the accuracy rate will always be saved). *Block Correction*—Disallow the use of the backspace, delete, and arrow keys. *Blackout Timing View*—Blackens the timing screen until timing is complete. *One Space / Two Space*—Set spacing after punctuation (".", ":", "!", "?").

TIMINGS	ERRORS ALLOWED	Block Correction	Blackout Timing View
15-Second	____	☐	☐
30-Second	____	☐	☐
1-Minute	____	☐	☐
2-Minute	____	☐	☐
3-Minute	____	☐	☐
4-Minute	____	☐	☐
5-Minute	____	☐	☐

● One Space   ○ Two Space

Timing Weights: There are timings of different lengths in each lesson. Your instructor may feel that 1, 2, or 3 minute timings should be weighted more heavily for grading purposes than 15 or 30 second timings. These weights are all ratio based. In the example below, 15-sec. timings have a value of 1; 30-sec. timings are worth 2 times as much as 15-sec. timings; 1, 2, and 3 minute timings are worth 3 times as much as 15-second timings. The weighted score will appear above each lesson on the *Progress Report*.

TIMINGS	TIMING WEIGHT	EXAMPLE
15-Second	____	1
30-Second	____	2
1-Minute	____	3
2-MInute	____	3
3-Minute	____	3
4-Minute	____	3
5-Minute	____	3

15-Second Timings

Warmup (All Letters Used)

1. A dozen women quivered when the snake caught the mouse.

2. Before you relax, please be sure your doors are locked.

Learn the 7 Key   **Reach with the J Finger**

3. jjj 777 jjj 777 jjj 777 jjj 777 jj7 jj7 77j 77j jj7 jj7

4. jar 777 jut 777 job 777 jaw 777 jam 777 jab 777 jet 777

5. There were 77 dancers, 777 singers, and 7 alto singers.

Learn the 8 Key   **Reach with the K Finger**

6. kkk 888 kkk 888 kkk 888 kk8 kk8 88k 88k k88 k88 kkk 888

7. cake 888 kicker 888 know 888 knit 888 kept 888 keel 888

8. My 88 kinfolk in the mountains cut 888 logs in 8 hours.

Learn the 9 Key   **Reach with the L Finger**

9. lll 999 lll 999 lll 999 ll9 ll9 99l 99l lll 999 lll 999

10. lot 999 let 999 lie 999 lug 999 lad 999 all 999 lap 999

11. Larry shot 99 bullets at the 19 big ducks and killed 9.

Learn the 0 Key   **Reach with the ; Finger**

12. ;;; 000 ;;; 000 ;;; 000 ;;; 000 ;;; 000 ;;; 000 ;;; 000

13. 000 ;;; 00; 00; ;;0 ;;0 000 ;;; 000 ;;; 0;; 0;; ;00 ;00

14. How do 10 healthy children sound so like 500 sometimes?

SETUP—Continued

Sections: These are the lessons to be included in grading; weight them as a percentage of the total grade. This also allows the course to be individualized for students or classes. Any lessons with a weight of 0% (or blank) will not be used in the *Final Grade Report*.

LESSONS	% OF TOTAL GRADE	EXAMPLE
1 - 13 (Alphabet A to M)	____	30%
14 - 26 (Alphabet N to Z)	____	30%
27 (All Letters)	____	5%
28 - 29 (Punctuation)	____	5%
30 - 34 (Numbers & Symbols)	____	5%
35 (All Letters)	____	5%
36 (All Letters)	____	5%
37 (All Letters)	____	5%
38 (All Letters)	____	5%
39 (All Letters)	____	5%
40 (All Letters)	____	0%
41 (All Letters)	____	0%

Grading Scale:

OVERALL AVERAGE WPM	GRADE	EXAMPLES
____	A	(50+)
____	B	(43)
____	C	(35)
____	D	(30)

Recap: The Recap screen shows you all the course standards that have been entered as a final check. If you have made an error, go back to the appropriate tab and enter the correct data. After you leave the *Setup*, **no changes can be made to the Name or ID.**

INTRODUCTION

Read each screen in the *Introduction*. It will introduce you to: the home row, how timings work, additional features of the program, and let you take some short practice timings.

15.   On a very stormy night many years ago an elderly
man and his wife entered the lobby of a small hotel in
Philadelphia. All the rooms were rented all over town
because of three conventions. The clerk didn't want to
send the elderly couple out in the rain with nowhere to
go, so he offered to let them share his room. The
couple at first objected, but the clerk insisted and
assured them that he was happy to do it. The next
morning, when they paid their bill, the man told the
clerk that he should be the manager of the best hotel
in the United States and maybe, someday, he would build
one for him. The clerk looked at the man and his wife
and smiled. Then he helped them with their bags. Two
years passed. One day he received a letter with a round
-trip ticket to New York. The elderly man requested
that he pay them a visit. When the clerk arrived in New
York, the old man led him to the corner of Fifth Avenue
and Thirty-fourth Street and pointed to a snazzy new
building that looked like a mansion. The elderly man
explained that the building was ready for him to
manage. The clerk thought he was joking. He wasn't. The
man's name was William Waldorf Astor and the hotel was
the original Waldorf-Astoria. The young clerk who
became its first manager was George C. Boldt.

LESSONS MENU

At the main menu, double click on *Lessons*. All the lessons will appear (*in demo/evaluation mode, not all lessons are available*). You will notice an empty box next to each lesson assigned in the Setup. This is lesson tracking. As each lesson is completed, a check mark will appear in the box.

Lesson timings can be printed by clicking on the printer icon after your timing has finished. This will print your name, ID, date/time, timing data keyed, errors underlined, WPM score, and errors made. This is especially helpful for in-class tests and may be required by your instructor to verify that students are 'doing their own work'. The printout may be compared to scores on the progress report.

If you already have some keyboarding skills you can take the **Course Entry** timing when starting the lessons and then take the **Course Exit** timing when finished. You will easily be able to see your skill improvements. **Course Entry** and **Course Exit** timings use Optional Timing 1 and Optional Timing 2, respectively, for these skill measurements if required.

Click on lesson '1 - A Key', and practice to increase your score. Your best three scores will always show below the timing screen. Your best score that meets the accuracy rate will be used in grading.

The timer begins when the first key is pressed: If you complete the line before the timer stops you, press the Enter key and begin again on the same line. Keep typing until the timer stops you! If you 'mess up' and want to start over, just click on the Timer button to restart the timing. Single line timings do not word wrap. Press the Enter key twice after finishing a paragraph and start again—keep typing. Paragraph timings will word wrap, use the Enter key twice between paragraphs and after finishing all paragraphs—and then start again.

The *Progress Report* will show an asterisk by any score in which the correction key was used: If you are in a classroom situation, ask your instructor if you can use the Backspace key to correct errors. The asterisks will be ignored if you are allowed to use the correction key. Learn to use the correction key quickly and efficiently so you do not waste time and lower your speed score.

Free Form

This allows you to be timed and receive a WPM score based on your own (or instructor-given) text. No error checking is performed since the program does not have your data. You will be prompted to enter the length of the timing.

15-Second Timings

Warmup (All Letters Used)

1. She paid Lanz to fix the ivory box that blew away then.

2. The bird squawked as Maci gave Jim money to pay for it.

Learn the 3 Key   **Reach with the D Finger**

3. ddd 333 ddd 333 ddd eee 333 ddd eee 333 d3d d3d 33d 33d

4. dab 333 dam 333 sad 333 bad 333 had 333 dog 323 ads 323

5. The 33 soldiers raided the 133 towns in 23 small areas.

Learn the 4 Key   **Reach with the F Finger**

6. fff rrr 444 fff rrr 444 f4f f4f rr4 rr4 44r 44r 44f 44f

7. 44 far 44 fun 41 fan 41 fad 42 fad 42 fin 43 fee 43 for

8. Today, 44 dogs barked, 34 cats howled; and 4 fish swam.

Learn the 5 Key   **Reach with the F Finger**

9. 555 fff 555 fff 555 fff f55 f55 55f 55f 5ff 5ff fff 555

10. 55 fox 55 fog 545 fib 545 fro 535 fit 535 fat 525 fly 5

11. There were 55 foxes, 45 bears, 5 pigs, and 15 big cats.

Learn the 6 Key   **Reach with the J Finger**

12. jjj 666 jjj 666 jjj 666 jjj 666 j6j j6j 66j 66j j6j j6j

13. 65 jar 65 jam 61 joy 61 jaw 62 job 62 jet 63 jug 63 jut

14. Mom made 65 jars of jam in 6 hours. Sara made 16 more.

There are two types of progress reports, *Simple* and *Comprehensive*. *Simple Reports* show the highest score for each lesson line (if lessons are re-done, higher scores will replace lower scores). *Comprehensive Reports* show the top three scores for every timing. When a lesson is complete, the average score for that lesson will show below the lesson number. Asterisks (*) indicate a correction key was used (Backspace, Delete, or Arrow keys). If correction is not allowed, you can replace the marked score by repeating the timing and beating the score without using the correction key. These reports can be printed by clicking on the printer icon. Below is a partial example of a *Simple Report*:

Skillbuilding Mastery—Progress Report

Proof Readings: P1: 100%   P2: 100%   P3: 90%   P4: 90%   P5: 100%   Avg: 96%

Name: Audra Owens ID#: ao123   Date: 12/16/20xx   6:47 PM

Lesson	1	2	3	4	5	6	7	8	9	10	11
Line Avg	54	50	52	53	55	50	59	63	54	63	55
1	66/0	52/1	62/0	45/0	58/1	50/0*	46/0*	53/0	58/0	51/1	54/0
2	61/1*	49/0	52/0	54/0	55/0	59/0*	45/0	54/0	58/0	60/0	55/1
3	55/0	53/0	46/0	77/0	62/0	47/0*	45/0	60/0*	53/1	51/0	55/0
4	49/0	49/0	50/0	45/0	53/1*	45/0*	50/0	50/0	46/1	45/0*	49/0
5	54/0	47/0	56/0*	47/0	55/0*	48/0	49/0	68/1	45/0	54/0	58/0
6	46/0	50/0	54/0*	54/1	55/0*	58/0	45/0	56/0	44/0	50/0	54/1
7	49/0	54/0	47/0	62/0	52/0	41/0	39/0	62/0	54/0*	49/1	56/0
8	50/0	37/0	62/0*	55/0	53/0	53/0	63/1*	58/0	55/0	54/1	53/0
9	60/0	48/0	50/0	44/0	48/0	48/0	53/0*	57/1	52/0	46/0	59/0
10	64/0	59/0	58/0	43/1	66/1*	47/0	66/1*	72/0	51/0	73/0*	61/0
11	51/0*	56/0	45/0	46/0	56/0	44/1	71/0	63/0	58/0	74/0	64/0
12	46/1*	47/0	25/0	60/0	48/2*	46/0	67/0	70/0	48/1*	71/0	45/0
13	47/0	49/2*	50/0	57/0	62/0	51/1	77/0	60/2	49/3*	67/0	45/2*
14	58/0	58/1	61/0	56/3	51/1	50/0	63/1	73/2	49/0	84/0	74/1
15	56/0	52/0	50/0	57/1	55/0	53/0	79/0	75/0	76/0	64/0	50/0

Lesson	12	13	14	15	16	17	18	19	20	21	22
Line Avg	56	57	60	57	57	53	58	58	62	59	61
1	58/0	51/0	51/0	49/0*	45/0*	44/0	58/0	60/0	46/0	47/0	54/1
2	57/0	54/0	51/0	51/0	51/0*	44/0	63/0	59/0	62/0	57/0	51/0
3	53/0	50/0	48/1	52/0	50/0*	47/1	60/0*	63/0	56/1	60/0	70/0
4	64/0	46/0	48/0	45/0	44/0*	44/0	63/0	61/0	57/0	51/0	66/0*
5	55/0*	54/0	61/1	53/0	49/0	49/0	62/0	51/1*	66/1	54/0*	63/0
6	49/0*	45/0	45/0	45/0	53/0	48/0	67/0	57/0*	60/0	46/0*	61/0
7	54/0	56/0*	46/0	52/0	48/1	32/0	22/2*	57/1*	54/0	73/0	70/1
8	52/0*	45/0	56/0	41/0*	45/0	40/0	61/1	60/0	67/0	52/0*	53/1
9	46/1	40/1*	48/2	48/0*	48/1	22/0*	51/0	61/0	68/2	46/1	69/0
10	50/0*	51/2	54/0	28/0	46/0	54/0*	61/0*	12/0*	63/0	52/1	57/0
11	56/1	52/0*	57/1	54/0*	45/0	63/0	63/0*	47/0	65/0*	66/2	68/0
12	49/1	48/0*	50/0	46/0	49/2*	45/0*	67/0	72/0	71/0	53/0	59/0
13	22/0	53/0	49/0	50/0	45/1	52/0	76/0	67/2*	70/0	55/0	69/1*
14	80/0	84/0*	92/2*	75/0	73/0	66/0	51/0	62/1	64/0	71/0	61/0*
15	67/0	67/0	54/1	67/0	67/0	62/0	61/0	61/0	61/0	61/0	57/1*

15.   One of the pitfalls people over forty fall into is
the thinking that it's too late for them to succeed.
Some years ago a man over sixty was offered nearly two
hundred thousand dollars for his restaurant-motel-
service station business that he had spent his life
building up. He turned down the offer because he loved
his business and didn't feel ready to retire. Two years
later, at age sixty-five, he was flat broke with
nothing but a Social Security check each month. The
state had built a new highway along a different route.
Most people would be crushed. He refused to give up.
Instead, he took stock of his abilities. He knew he
could fry chicken, and do it well. He bade his wife
good-bye and, in a battered old car, set off equipped
with a pressure cooker, a can of specially prepared
flour, and much zeal. He set out to sell his secret
recipe and idea for frying chicken to other
restaurants. It was tough going and he often slept in
the car because he didn't have enough money for a hotel
room. His idea caught on and his hard work paid off. A
few years later, he built a nationwide franchised chain
of Kentucky Fried Chicken. The man was none other than
the jovial Colonel Sanders.

The *Current Grade Report* shows the average WPM for all consecutively completed lessons. The final grade on the final grade report may differ slightly due to the weights of each section into the total grade (see 'Sections' in the Setup). If your current grade or final grade is not satisfactory to you, view your *Progress Report* to identify those timing scores that need more practice. A higher score will replace a lower score of the same lesson and line number. This report can be printed by clicking on the printer icon.

Skillbuilding Mastery—Current Grade Report

Name: Audra Owens   ID#: ao123   Date: 05/06/20xx   9:15 AM

```
        Grading Scale:  50+    =   A

                        43     =   B

                        35     =   C

                        30     =   D

                        Below  =   F


        Your AVERAGE ^UNWEIGHTED^ WPM SCORE is: 47
  This grade report is the average of 13 lessons completed.
```

15-Second Timings

Warmup (All Letters Used)

1. Jason is lazy and won't move the queen to another hive.

2. The biker failed to exercise caution before going home.

Infrequently Used Symbols — ^, <, >
Practice the ^ Key   Use the J Finger & Shift of the 6 Key

3. ^^^ jjj ^^^ jjj ^^^ jjj ^^^ jjj ^^^ jjj ^^^ jjj ^^^ jjj

4. Is 6^6 too big a number? It is probably more than 6^1.

Practice the < Key   Use the K Finger & Shift of the , Key

5. <<< kkk <<< kkk <<< kkk <<< kkk <<< kkk <<< kkk <<< kkk

6. 2 is less than 3, and is shown by 2<3; and 4<5 and 6<7.

Practice the > Key   Use the L Finger & Shift of the . Key

7. >>> lll >>> lll >>> lll >>> lll >>> lll >>> lll >>> lll

8. 5 is greater than 4, and is shown by 5>4; and 5>3, too.

Numbers — 1, 2
Practice the 1 Key   Reach with the A Finger

9. aaa qqq 111 qqq aaa 111 qqq aaa qqq 111 qqq 111 qqq aaa

10. 11 qua 111 aqua 11 also 111 ail 11 ant 111 ash 11 are 1

11. There was 111 bees in this hive; there are only 11 now.

Practice the 2 Key   Use the ; Finger & Shift of the 0 Key

12. sss www 222 sss www 222 sss 222 sss 222 sss www 222 www

13. 12 stab 12 sat 121 sad 121 shy 122 saw 212 saw 212 star

14. We watched 122 shooting stars. There were 12 big ones.

The *Final Grade Report* shows the total weighted WPM for all completed lessons and sections. This final grade and WPM score may differ slightly from the *Current Grade Report* score due to weights being applied to section scores (see 'Sections' in the *Setup*). This report can be printed by clicking on the printer icon.

Keyboard Mastery—Evaluation and Grade Report

```
Name: Audra Owens                    ** Final Timing Grade:  A
ID#:  ao123                             Total Weighted WPM:  55
Time: 10:44 AM            ***All lessons assigned in the SETUP must be
Date: 05/06/20xx          completed before a final grade will appear.
```

Course Entry Score: 35   Course Exit Score: 61   Improvement: 26

Spacing: One Space

Errors Allowed:		**Block Correction:**	
15-Sec. Timing = 0		15-Sec. Timing = Yes	
30-Sec. Timing = 1		30-Sec. Timing = Yes	
1-Min. Timing = 1		1-Min. Timing = No	
2-Min. Timing = 2		2-Min. Timing = No	
3-Min. Timing = 3		3-Min. Timing = No	
4-Min. Timing = 4		4-Min. Timing = No	
5-Min. Timing = 5		5-Min. Timing = No	

Timing Weights:		**Grading Scale:**		
15-Sec. Timing = 1		50+	=	A
30-Sec. Timing = 2		43	=	B
1-Min. Timing = 3		35	–	C
2-Min. Timing = 3		30	=	D
3-Min. Timing = 3		Below	=	F
4-Min. Timing = 3				
5-Min. Timing = 3				

Section	Avg. Score	X	% of Total	=	WPM Score
1–13 Alphabet A to M	55	X	30%	=	16.5
14–26 Alphabet N to Z	57	X	30%	=	17.1
27 All Letters	47	X	5%	=	2.35
28–29 Punctuation	59	X	5%	=	2.95
30–34 Numbers & Symbols	49	X	5%	=	2.45
31 All Letters	48	X	5%	=	4.4
32 All Letters	46	X	5%	=	2.3
33 All Letters	46	X	5%	=	2.3
34 All Letters	52	X	5%	=	2.6
35 All Letters	52	X	0%	=	0
36 All Letters	57	X	0%	=	0
37 All Letters	57	X	0%	=	0
38 All Letters	57	X	5%	=	2.85
39 All Letters	54	X	0%	=	0
40 All Letters	59	X	0%	=	0
41 All Letters	59	X	0%	=	0
				Total WPM:	55.40

15.   An airline executive was tired of constant problems
    with people. He longed for perfect employees. He was
    quite delighted when scientists suggested replacing air
    crews with completely automatic planes. Computers would
    replace pilots, engineers, and even flight attendants.
    No more errors, no more emotional difficulties, no more
    people problems.

         A demonstration flight was arranged. Everything was
    perfect: the plane zoomed off, reached cruising
    altitude, and leveled off. A voice came over the
    speaker system and announced a welcome. It said that
    lunch would be served. After lunch the computer
    suggested that the passengers sit back and enjoy the
    flight. It continued by telling them that nothing can
    go wrong, nothing can go wrong, nothing can go wrong,
    nothing can go wrong... The point is that few things in
    this world are perfect. A good leader knows how to
    handle human errors without making employees feel like
    failures. As a general rule, excellent work does not
    come from people who view themselves as failures.
    Consider the time and effort that has been put into
    their work. None of us should be considered incompetent
    because we don't always turn in absolutely perfect
    work.

SECTION B

Lessons 1-41
- The S.E.C.R.E.T. to successful keyboarding
- Directions for Course Entry & Course Exit timings
    - 5-Minute Course Entry timing
    - 5-Minute Course Exit timing
- Drills from A-Z with Speed and Accuracy
- Punctuation
- Symbols
- Numbers
- More 5-Minute Timings

15-Second Timings

     Warmup (All Letters Used)

1. If you bake an extra dozen quiches, we won't take them.

2. Opal joked that our pizza was already given to the zoo.

     Practice the & Key   **Use the J Finger & Shift of the 7 Key**

3. jjj &&& jjj &&& jjj &&& jjj &&& j&& j&& &&j &&j jjj &&&

4. jab &&& got &&& sit &&& ate &&& bit &&& pal &&& rum &&&

5. chevrolet & pontiac; boots & pail; black & white; 7 & 7

     Practice the * Key   **Use the K Finger & Shift of the 8 Key**

6. *** kkk *** kkk *** kkk k** k** **k **k k*k k*k kkk ***

7. *forest* *stand* *top* *spill* *catch* *carry* *quarry*

8. Emphasize these words this way: *store* *brand* *sale*

     Practice the (Key   **Use the L finger & Shift of the 9 Key**

9. (((lll (((lll (((lll (((lll ((l ((l ll(ll((((lll

10. l((l((((l ((l lll (((lll (((lll (((lll (((lll (((

11. truck (((cars (((ever (((story (((easy (((hard (((

     Practice the) Key   **Use the ; Finger & Shift of the 0 Key**

12.))) ;;;))) ;;;))) ;;;))) ;;;))) ;;;))) ;;;))) ;;;

13.));)); ;;) ;;)))) ;;;))) ;;; ;)) ;)));;);; ;;;)))

14. (the) (cat) (were) (talent) (travel) (soft) (hard) (be)

The **S.E.C.R.E.T.** to Successful Keyboarding Skills

S — SIT upright, arms and wrists straight.

E — Keep your EYES on the copy.

C — Use CORRECT fingers.

R — Keep a reasonable RHYTHM.

E — Eliminate ERRORS properly.
> If your teacher allows error correction, keep your 'J' finger on the 'J' key while your little finger depresses the 'backspace' key.

T — TAP your keys as if they were hot!

Directions for the Course Entry/Exit Timings

In order for you to know how much you have improved by the end of this course, it is necessary to take a **Course Entry** and **Course Exit** timing. The purpose of this course is to prepare you for employment. Most typing employment tests are 5-minutes long with limited errors. Therefore, our entry and exit timings are 5-minutes using the error limit for 5-minute timings as set in the 'Setup' (*see the 'Options' tab on the 'Setup' screen*).

After completion of the course, take the **Course Exit** timing. You will be thrilled with your improvement! Your **Course Entry** and **Course Exit** scores, and your **Improvement**, will display on your Final Grade Report. Carefully follow the directions below:

1. Only timings that meet the accuracy rate assigned in the setup will be saved. You may take the timings several times. Get at least one timing saved that you feel best reflects your typing ability at this point.
2. Use the tab key for the 5-space paragraph indentation.
3. You may use the correction keys to correct mistakes if allowed by your instructor (an asterisk '*' will appear next to any timing that correction was used).
4. The paragraph lines look spaced just to make it easier to read. The timing is actually single spaced.
5. Paragraph timings word wrap automatically. If you finish the paragraph before the time is up: (1) press the Enter key twice to double space, and (2) indent and begin the paragraph again.

15.   Try to be understanding in your judgment of others. Everyone makes mistakes sometimes, so don't be too harsh about them. It may seem superior, smart, and clever to be critical, but it's a poor way to make or keep friends. It never accomplishes as much as a friendly, understanding reminder. Sharp criticism makes people angry, not sorry.

         Jeff was a small boy who attended a summer camp. One day he received a large package of dozens of cookies in the mail from his mother. After eating some, he put them under his bed. The next day they were gone. The camp counselor told Jeff that she knew who took them. She advised him to ask his mother for another box of cookies. When the cookies arrived, she told Jeff to go to the boy and share the cookies with him. At first he didn't want to do it. After all, the other kid stole his cookies in the first place. The counselor quietly persuaded Jeff to share. Soon, the two boys were arm in arm and the boy was trying to get Jeff to accept his jackknife in payment for the stolen cookies. Sometimes we need to let the other person save face. Life becomes friendlier and more enjoyable if you learn to forgive and forget. Those who don't learn this miss out on the warmth and friendships they might enjoy.

Quite often simple praise inspires a person to change and improve, and can be the biggest influence for success in the future. In the early nineteenth century, a young man in London aspired to be a writer. However, everything seemed to be against him. He had only four years of schooling. His father had been in jail because he couldn't pay his debts. This young man knew hunger pangs well. Finally, he got a job in a warehouse infested with rats and roaches affixing labels on bottles of blacking. He slept at night in a dismal attic room with two other boys from the slums of London. He had so little confidence in his ability to write that he sneaked out and mailed his first manuscript in the dead of night so the others wouldn't laugh at him. Story after story was rejected. Finally the great day came when one was accepted. There was no money in it for him, but the editor paused to write him a note of praise. He was so thrilled that he said he walked aimlessly around the streets with tears rolling down his cheeks. The praise and recognition that the editor gave him changed his whole life. It was that encouragement, which he prized, that prompted him to continue writing. You probably have heard of that boy. His name was Charles Dickens. His stories are the literature of many English classes.

15-Second Timings

Warmup (All Letters Used)

1. A jury acquitted Zeb of avoiding paying his income tax.

2. Kent works at a car wash and waxes the clean, new cars.

Practice the @ Key   Use the S Finger & Shift of the 2 Key

3. sss @@@ sss @@@ sss @@@ sss @@@ sss @@@ sss @@@ sss @@@

4. @@s @@s ss@ ss@ s@@ s@@ @ss @ss @@@ sss @@@ sss s@@ s@@

5. @@@ sad @@@ sit @@@ sac @@@ sub @@@ sob @@@ ash @@@ has

Practice the # Key   Use the D Finger & Shift of the 3 Key

6. ### ddd ### ddd ### ddd ##d ##d dd# dd# ### ddd ### ddd

7. ### did ### doe ### aid ### add ### dot ### dud ### dab

8. Did #50 song ever make it ahead of #35? Or was it #56?

Practice the $ Key   Use the F finger & Shift of the 4 Key

9. $$$ fff $$$ fff $$$ fff $$$ fff $$$ fff $$$ fff $$$ fff

10. $$f $$f ff$ ff$ $$f $$f ff$ ff$ $ff $ff f$$ f$$ fff $$$

11. Bob paid $5.00; it shouldn't have been more than $4.00.

Practice the % Key   Use the F Finger & Shift of the 5 Key

12. %%% fff %%% fff %%% fff %%% fff %%% fff %%% fff %%% fff

13. %%f %%f ff% ff% f%% f%% %%f %%f fff %%% fff %%% f%% f%%

14. The rate always has a % sign, such as 15% or 10% or 5%.

When the first Marshall Field was building his department store into one of Chicago's finest stores, he spent a lot of time each working day visiting each floor and observing everything. One day a little girl and her mother were observed shopping. The little girl was excited as she was telling another child that her daddy ran one of the departments in the Field store. She talked about her daddy's store and her daddy's department as if he actually owned a part of it. Suddenly, the little girl's mother recognized Marshall Field standing in the aisle listening to the children talk. The mother started to apologize for her daughter. She feared that he might possibly take offense at what he heard. Marshall Field, with a wave of his hand, assured her that he was quite pleased. He said that he wanted her father to feel that it was his store, and he wanted her father to feel that it was his department, and not just a job. Marshall Field felt that if he could induce every employee to feel that way, he wouldn't have to be concerned about the success of his business. Think about it. The biggest mistake you can make is to believe that you are working for someone else. Marshall Field knew the truth of that statement and attributes a good amount of his success to helping his employees feel they are an important part of the business.

15.   Henry Kaiser said that a problem is opportunity in work clothes. People who will spend extra effort to solve problems will most often reap benefits in the future that they never imagined. Years ago two brothers, Thaddeus and Erastus Fairbanks, were running a small hemp business. Their biggest difficulty was in trying to weigh the hemp with the crude and inaccurate scales available at that time. Eventually, Thaddeus devised a platform scale which solved their problem. What happened after that came as a complete surprise. Many of their customers wanted to buy their scales more than they wanted to buy hemp. As a favor to these customers, the two brothers made more scales. Soon the demand for their scales was so great that they quit the hemp business. Their new venture led them to enjoy an amazing fortune beyond their wildest dreams. This all came about because they had the courage and ambition to tackle a problem to try to find a solution. Natural talent, intelligence, a wonderful education--none of these guarantee success. Something else is needed: the sensitivity to understand what other people want and the willingness to work to give it to them. Worldly success depends on pleasing others.

The timer will begin when you strike the first key. If you "mess up", you may stop the timer and start over by clicking on the Timer button. You may take as many timings as necessary to achieve your goal. Only those scores that meet the accuracy rate as shown in the Setup will be saved (see 'Options' tab in Setup). The best three scores for each line will record so you and your instructor can see improvement. The best speed for each line is used in calculating your lesson average.

Each line is a separate timing. If you finish the line before the time is up, press the 'Enter' key and start the same line again (paragraph timings word wrap and do not require striking the 'Enter' key at the end of the timing). Keep typing until you hear the beep or see the screen blink which signals the end of the timing.

15-Second Timings

1. all all add add sal sal aha aha ask ask ail ail sad sad

2. arm arm alm alm pad pad dad dad Sam Sam was was and and

3. ace ace apt apt all all are are add add ash ash Ann Ann

4. adds adds raid raid rare rare sale sale tale tale fades

5. ails ails Adam Adam asks asks lake lake tare tare dares

30-Second Timings

6. area area afar afar bear bear gala gala papa papa doors

7. pagan pagan array array salad salad arena arena appears

8. banana banana sauna sauna atlas atlas canal canal quick

9. Ann will give a new car to the first one that asks her.

10. Adam plans to ask her for a date to the prom real soon.

1-Minute Timings

11. The awards will go to the animal with the best manners.

12. Will Amy eat the banana and papaya at the annual party?

15-Second Timings

    Warmup (All Letters Used)

1. Quiet Mike had a big party in Juarez over this weekend.

2. Can Florence have the axe to use to chop oak fire wood?

    Practice the , Key   **Reach with the K Finger**

3. arm, job, are, you, the, his, ran, one, day, the, star,

4. clam, wolf, lazy, told, pert, snap, veal, axle, blares,

5. Yes, I want the shirt, socks, and underwear washed too.

    Practice the ? Key   **Use the Shift of the / Key**

6. who? what? when? where? now? then? here? there? who me?

At the end of a sentence, space once or twice after question marks (depending on setup).

7. is it? why not? over there? Jack will? Sara won't? why?

8. Will Mary come to the party? Did you speak to Jeffrey?

    Practice the / Key   **Reach with the ; Finger**

9. here/there up/down go/come yes/no true/false three/four

10. one/two five/six seven/eight eleven/twelve thirty/forty

11. Ky's test had some yes/no and true/false answers on it.

    Practice the ! Key   **Use the Shift of the 1 Key**

12. !!! aaa !!! aaa !!! aaa !!! aaa a!! a!! !!a !!a aaa 111

13. stop! go! wait! help! no! yes! forget it! Don't! Don't!

At the end of a sentence, space once or twice after exclamation marks (depending on setup).

14. Stop the train! Help her now! Don't go yet! Heck no!

13. Carla was on top of the canal bank when the water came.

14. Darr is amazed that the animals appear to be so active.

15. Andy is aware that an appeal for data will appall Jack.

Take a moment to view your Progress Report by double-clicking on Progress Reports in the software menu and then choose 'Simple Report'. Do you see your scores?

You may also notice a square box next to many lessons in the 'Lessons Menu'. These boxes show which lessons have been assigned in the 'Setup'. When all lines in an assigned lesson have a score recorded, a checkmark will appear in these boxes showing lessons completed.

15.   Stores often use soothing background music to make
customers relax and possibly buy more. Psychological
research has shown that the auditory environment can
have as great an effect on employees as the visual one.
Imagine working with a background of funeral music or
slow, mournful sounds. Yet, a background that is too
noisy is just as distracting. Studies have shown that
people need noise up to a point, though the same
background noise can be soothing to one and distracting
to another. Do you recall a time when everything was so
quiet that you felt something was wrong? We all tend to
get used to a certain noise level and feel comfortable
with it. On one job, a production supervisor complained
that her office was too quiet. She had grown up in the
Bronx, New York, near a subway line. To her, the quiet
was distracting. Another manager had an office next to
the milling machine room and couldn't stand the
constant buzz of the machinery. He grew up on a quiet
sheep ranch. To him, the noise was distracting. Not
only was the noise level wrong for both employees, but
the difficulties in concentration lowered their
productivity. When the two managers switched offices,
everything was fine.

Be sure to keep your eyes on the book, not on your fingers!

Strike the keys lightly and quickly—as if they were hot.

15-Second Timings

1. rub rub lab lab sub sub bud bud bus bus bit bit rib rib

2. bar bar bad bad bib bib ban ban bed bed big big bat bat

3. cub cub ebb ebb bil bil bet bet bud bud dub dub tab tab

4. robe robe buff buff stub stub boat boat butt butt barbs

5. blab blab blob blob crab crab blew blew baby baby boots

30-Second Timings

6. bulb bulb blue blue ball ball gabs gabs bank bank brats

7. cabby cabby lobby lobby abbey abbey bribe bribe ribbons

8. bobbins bobbins cabbage cabbage rabbits rabbits nibbled

9. The boy bobbed for balls in the black tub at the party.

10. The comb was big and blue; and a bargain at that price.

1-Minute Timings

11. Baby rabbits nibbled at the big cabbage near the brook.

12. He bragged about his hobby of making bamboo bird cages.

13. The barber grabbed his big comb before it hit the bowl.

14. Barry bragged and blew bubbles to amuse all the babies.

15. She had a hobby of tying ribbons on boards tinted blue.

15-Second Timings

Warmup (All Letters Used)

1. Marj arranged five dozen exotic baskets with wax paper.

2. Holly quit her job early so we could all go to the zoo.

Practice the - Key   **Reach with the ; Finger**

3. The- good- natured- typist- always- was- on- time- too-

4. self-controlled first-class on-the-job two-way red-hots

5. My baby-sitter is good-natured and a self-starter here.

Practice the : Key   **Use the Shift of ; Key**

6. follows: ahead: reports: below: check: equip: to:

7. To: From: Date: Subject: mail: dates: cars: job:

8. The game will be played at: Chandler and Gilbert High.

Practice the ' Key   **Reach with the ; Finger**

9. can't wouldn't couldn't don't wasn't weren't isn't I'll

10. They weren't mad; but they don't want us to win either.

11. He can't go at these times: mealtime or late evenings.

Practice the " Key   **Use the Shift of ' Key**

12. "and" "when" "were" "help" "fairy" "bread" "what isn't"

13. "my" "will" "read" "help" "fire" "play" "from" "thrill"

At the end of a sentence, space once or twice after quotation marks (depending on setup).

14. "He can't play." She wrote: "No dice." "Evans won't."

Are your wrists and arms level? Don't rest your wrists on the desk or bottom of the keyboard.

15-Second Timings

1. can can car car cot cot cam cam cdc cdc cow cow ace ace

2. cue cue caw caw cob cob cop cop cry cry con con cab cab

3. act act tic tic tac tac toc toc cad cad cub cub cyc cyc

4. cash cash coax coax cold cold club club coco coco check

5. cage cage cake cake camp camp cozy cozy comb comb civic

30-Second Timings

6. cost cost corn corn race race dice dice coal coal corps

7. cracks cracks occupy occupy chance chance tactic tactic

8. contact contact comic comic crucial crucial cubic cubic

9. Can Carol contact the old comic and draw up a contract?

10. The check for the cages was cashed at the civic center.

1-Minute Timings

11. Calories in creamed corn are a concern in strict diets.

12. The cocky chickens made quite a scene when a duck came.

13. The cranky baby had colic all night and kept all awake.

14. It is crucial that the oldest classic car be sold last.

15. A checkup can succeed in catching problems while small.

From Lesson 28 forward, only the 5-Minute timings are used for grading purposes. However, all exercises completed will appear on the Progress Report. Check with your instructor to see how many exercises should be completed.

Fast typists keep their fingers close to the home row. When you depress the Enter key, can you keep your 'j' finger on the 'j' key as a guide for the rest of the fingers to get back quickly to the home row? Try to depress the 'Enter' key and keep typing without skipping a beat.

15-Second Timings

1. dad dad dud dud dax dax ded ded had had lad lad duo duo

2. aid aid dab dab daz daz add add fad fad lid lid did did

3. cod cod dye dye die die and and ads ads dog dog dig dig

4. door door date date dude dude code code died died dread

5. fade fade bide bide darn darn deed deed adds adds domed

30-Second Timings

6. fads fads dash dash band band dote dote dyed dyed dance

7. drill drill dread dread idea idea dish dish deals deals

8. doodles doodles defined defined diamond diamond dwindle

9. Did Don doodle on the deed or did he doodle on a scrap?

10. Dad will send a daily order for good food to the diner.

1-Minute Timings

11. Did the ladies who bid on diamonds decide to bid later?

12. David did dare to see the lawyers and defend our deeds.

13. Eddy is saddened to hear it was decided to call it off.

14. Darin defied the building code and arranged a new deal.

15. The address was faded but the saddle did get delivered.

15.   A lack of responsibility and initiative is a
familiar problem among managers who delegate. Perhaps
the problem is understanding effective delegation. It
is stimulating to be asked to help solve a tough
problem; it is positively boring to be told exactly how
to do a job in every detail. Herein lies the chief
difference between good delegation and bad. General
George Patton concurs: Don't tell a man how to do a
thing. Tell him what you want done, and he will
surprise you with his ingenuity. It's a good rule to
follow. When you give workers a job to do, take care to
tell what, when, and why you want it done. But don't
take the pizazz out of it by telling them how. Don't
squash initiative. Let them figure it out for
themselves and feel involved in the process. They may
also contribute some good ideas you didn't think of.

     Is the work too critical to take a chance on
delegating it? Then why not delegate it with close
supervision? Ask the subordinate to figure out the best
method, then check with you before proceeding. Leaders
who delegate wisely are the ones who develop capable
and judicious subordinates. It's the best sign that
they themselves are ready to move ahead up the
corporate ladder.

The best way to gain speed is to eliminate pauses. Go at a comfortable, steady rate.

15-Second Timings

1. ded ded eye eye eel eel see see ego ego bee bee tee tee

2. eat eat elf elf wee wee err err egg egg eve eve fee fee

3. elf elf ale ale led led eke eke elm elm met met tel tel

4. seek seek sees sees seed seed else else ever ever geese

5. need need fees fees tree tree leak leak sake sake dames

30-Second Timings

6. dells dells desks desks earn earn sled sled rakes rakes

7. three three enter enter elder elder embers embers seven

8. elected elected degree degree coffee coffee event event

9. The three elders decreed that they must lower expenses.

10. Seven enemy elements raided camp; eleven men were left.

1-Minute Timings

11. Nine emcees were elected to be in charge of the coffee.

12. I believe there are fewer verses to see in this decree.

13. They spent three weeks and added expenses to elect her.

14. Pete Green greeted the referees before three big games.

15. The beetle event was a success that exceeded our hopes.

15-Second Timings

1. dab jam irk fox evil socks quaint graphic sleazy cowboy

2. quit shock away vim dozen whiz axle paired judge buffet

3. Can Jon Waltz quickly pedal that bike five extra miles?

4. Bud Jemckins quit paying very awful taxes on his pizza.

5. Dave quickly won six major prizes for best high jumper.

6. Pawn Viker acquired wax gifts from lazy high jump boys.

7. Jmil was criticized except for heavy quarterback gains.

30-Second Timings

8. wax jinx waifs byte quiz mold hive kinky zircons gypped

9. wax pry kidd comb dozen jaunt quail savvy bought flavor

10. Marcy Pyl had vowed to quit sax in five big jazz bands.

11. Jozef Varghn gave jam and six quad lot copies of books.

12. Crazy Mox will quit juggling very fresh baked nut pies.

13. Berj analyzed data with five complex questions quickly.

14. Val Mikey paid Josh for high quiz scores on tax briefs.

PRACTICE WORDS FOR PARAGRAPH TIMING

responsibility responsibility initiative subordinates

delegation delegation stimulating stimulating solve

positively positively exactly exactly ingenuity Don't

FOR PRACTICE:

Read and circle all errors in the paragraph below. Errors include transposing and other misspellings and spacing. You should find 14 errors.

No mater how briliant a man may be otherwise, it it doesn't necessarily meen he'll also be a good manager. Managing peeple is a different kind of hall game. You would think that a fellow who knew every job in a department backwords and forwords would naturally make the best manager. Actually, he might have serious problems. In the first place, if he juges everyone else by his own standards, he may expec1 them to do a lot better than they are capible of doing. If he also insists on showing them how much better he can do their their jobs than they can, nobody's going to be iery happy working for him.

FOR REAL:

Correct all spelling and spacing errors below. Select 'Proof Reading 1' from the 'Proof Readings' menu. Type the paragraph. It will word wrap automatically to the next line as you type. Proofread carefully—there is a 10 point error penalty for every error. Only the first attempt will record.

Doing a job well yourself is one thing; pursuading others to do it well is another. When a man or woman moves into supervision or managment, they have crossed a significant line. They can no longerbe judged solely by what they can do by themselves. Thier value now depends mainly on what they can acomplish working through others. Every manager must delegate to others many things he/she could do better; however, it's best to keep that fact hidden. Couching and training people must be done tackfully--without flanting superiority or or undermining thier self-respect.

15.   If you want results in dealing with people, you have to let them know what is going on. Employees can't work efficiently or enthusiastically in a vacuum. Some bosses make a practice of excluding information, telling people only the minimum facts they need to handle their jobs. That is a serious mistake. Ignorance of the facts causes gossiping, and needless resentment. The smartest policy is to tell employees everything you possibly can with correct information so rumors don't have a chance to get a foothold. Once a decision is made about anything, the wisest course is to announce it as fast as you can before the grapevine buzzes and beats you to it. You like to be in on things. You like your supervisors to take you into their confidence and keep you informed. When they don't, it doesn't make you feel very important, or enthusiastic about cooperating.

     Good bosses try to keep their people fully informed at all times. It is an important part of their jobs, so they take it seriously and try to do it well. They know that when information quits, rumors start. They want cooperation, not just compliance; keeping people well informed promptly is essential to getting it.

Can you press the 'Enter' key at the end of a line quickly and keep typing without pausing? This is real important to gaining good speed.

15-Second Timings

1. foe foe for for fad fad fig fig fog fog fun fun fox fox

2. fan fan fin fin fat fat fix fix fee fee fib fib fur fur

3. fiv fiv fir fir fit fit fry fry fom fom fad fad fie fie

4. fell fell buff buff five five four four fend fend affix

5. fifth fifth staff staff offset offset fitful fitful far

6. fearful fearful riffraff riffraff offenses offenses fat

30-Second Timings

7. fifty fifty taffy taffy bluff bluff affix affix baffles

8. affirm affirm fearful fearful frills frills fable fable

9. offices offices muffins muffins fulfill fulfill differs

10. Fran and her friends fixed waffles, muffins, and fudge.

11. Frank and Fred had fifty traffic offenses in Flagstaff.

12. Fearful officials shuffled five armfuls of old folders.

1-Minute Timings

13. Fay differs with her four friends on fixing soft taffy.

14. The French foresters followed that fox into the forest.

14.   We all like to be treated as if we are special and important. It makes us feel good. You probably would go the extra mile, so to speak, to give quality treatment to large customers or important prospects. But what about all the others? Small accounts have a way of eventually growing into bigger ones. One of your small buyers may quit and move to a bigger company. That little customer may give you a lucrative and important recommendation. Since you can't tell for sure which customers will benefit you the most in the long run, why not dazzle them all with special treatment? People enjoy doing business with people who make them feel special or important. They will avoid, if possible, doing business with those who make them feel unimportant. You can count on it.

PRACTICE WORDS FOR PARAGRAPH TIMING

efficiently efficiently ignorance ignorance gossiping

enthusiastically enthusiastically excluding excluding

grapevine grapevine buzzes buzzes supervisors informed

confidence confidence seriously seriously compliance

Before you take this next paragraph timing, take short timings on the practice words. These are words that have been selected because they most probably will slow you down. If you can type them quickly, you will get a much better score on the paragraph timing. You may select words or phrases of your own to practice.

You can open a special 'Drill Screen' by clicking on the Drill icon in the toolbar. This will allow you to practice the words below. If you finish the line, start over on the same line. Keep practicing each line until your speed and accuracy is satisfactory. You will need to proofread your timing yourself.

PRACTICE WORDS FOR PARAGRAPH TIMING

---

ninety ninety percent percent friction friction extra

amazed amazed argument argument dealing dealing cause

When typing paragraphs, depress the TAB key for the 5-space paragraph indention. It will automatically word wrap so you don't have to depress the 'Enter' key after each line. If you finish the paragraph before the time is up, press the 'Enter' key twice to double-space, indent, and begin again. Keep typing!

Check the 'Setup' to determine if you should space once or twice at the end of a sentence. The paragraph looks double-spaced to make it easier to read. You will actually be typing it in as single-spaced.

1-Minute Timing   **All Letters Used, S.I.—1.2**

15.   It has been said that ninety percent of the

extra friction of daily life is caused by the wrong

tone of voice. When dealing with people, be careful

of what you say with the tone of your voice, even in

jest. You may not mean what it says. If you raise

your voice in anger to make a point, don't be amazed

if a not so quiet argument occurs.

15-Second Timings

1. zoo zoo zee zee zip zip zap zap aza aza qaz qaz zac zac

2. zing zing fizz fizz zero zero buzz buzz lazy lazy zebra

3. pizza pizza frizz frizz seize seize plaza plaza puzzles

4. zigzag zigzag whizzed whizzed drizzle drizzle dozen zoe

5. citizens citizens buzzard buzzard zoomed zoomed muzzled

6. horizons horizons zoologist zoologist magazine magazine

7. Grizzlies zigzagged around the bulldozers in amazement.

30-Second Timings

8. zooms zooms zippy zippy gazed gazed snooze snooze sizes

9. dazzles dazzles zipped zipped snazzy snazzy zeros zeros

10. hazardous hazardous sneezing sneezing frenzied frenzied

11. Lazy zebras snoozed quietly among lizards and buzzards.

12. That wizard of zoology amazes zillions of zoo visitors.

13. The zealous citizens seized those lazy fuzzy grizzlies.

PRACTICE WORDS FOR PARAGRAPH TIMING

quality quality treatment treatment customers customers

eventually eventually lucrative lucrative dazzle dazzle

recommendation recommendation unimportant unimportant

15-Second Timings

1. gfg gfg gag gag get get got got tag tag gum gum gap gap

2. gun gun gab gab gal gal gin gin gob gob egg egg gav gav

3. wag wag lag lag igg igg gor gor gnu gnu gas gas sag sag

4. gang gang gave gave gear gear gift gift goat goat green

5. gouges gouges goggle goggle gargle gargle giggle giggle

6. giggling giggling debugging debugging eggnog eggnog sog

30-Second Timings

7. muggy muggy soggy soggy haggle haggle pegged pegged gog

8. games games garages garages luggage luggage garbage tag

9. jogging jogging suggest suggest baggage baggage giggles

10. Gregg suggested going to get our baggage after jogging.

11. Eggnog may gag some people but it is great before golf.

12. Grace is going to pick green grapes as a gift to Greta.

1-Minute Timings

13. The group thought jogging and giggling was greater fun.

14. Morgan likes biology, geology, ecology, and some Greek.

DIRECTIONS:

Select Proof Reading 5 from the Proof Readings menu. This is an exercise in proofreading and in following directions. Type the following personal business letter in block style, making all corrections. Proofread your typing carefully. There will be a penalty of 10 points for every error, spacing or spelling. Only the first attempt will record on the Progress Report.

Beginning on line 1, press the Enter key twelve times before typing the first line of your return address. Paragraphs will word wrap automatically, typed lines need not end exactly as shown.

```
(press return key 12 times for a 2" margin)


6489 North 16th Street

Phoenix, AZ 85103

Current Date (after date, press enter/return key 4 times)


Dr. Clifford Goodman

Chandler Community Hospital

678 S. Dobson Road

Chandler, Az 85224 (press enter/return key 2 times to double space)


Dear DR. Goodman,
     lc
We apologize for any inconvenience that you may have been caused by the
malfunction of the hard drive on your new MXV computer. The MXV has an
outstanding reputation for dependability and has an excellent performance
record. Occasionally, however, a computer does not function as it should.


     We have asked our service personnel to personally visit the
computer site and perform whatever repairs are necessary to be sure the
computer is working. If you have any other trouble with it, we will
replace it free of charge.
              properly
Thank you for your patience in this matter.

Sincerely yours,


MXV COMPUTERLAND (press enter/return key 4 times to name)



Ms. Irene Campbell (press enter/return key 2 times to reference initials)


IC/xx (Replace "xx" with your initials in lower case.)
```

Use the drill screen to practice the words below.

PRACTICE WORDS FOR PARAGRAPH TIMING

satisfaction satisfaction everyone's everyone's quest
freedom freedom people people managers managers thought
expertise expertise operation operation aspects aspects

Remember to check the 'Setup' to determine if you should space once or twice at the end of a sentence. The paragraph looks double-spaced to make it easier to read. You will actually be typing it in as single-spaced.

1-Minute Timing   **All Letters Used, S.I.—1.3**

15.   Job satisfaction is everyone's quest. The more
        freedom you can give people to do a job the way they
        would like to do it, the more job satisfaction they
        will get from it. Managers are thought of as having
        expertise in most aspects of the job. However, if
        you insist on doing all the thinking for your
        operation, and if every little thing has to be done
        your way, the zeal is taken out of it. What is left
        for your people to be proud of?

15.   The big secret of dealing with people is to learn to get people to want to do what needs to be done. The best way to accomplish this is to give people what they want. The deepest principle in human nature is the craving to be appreciated. It was this desire for a feeling of importance that led an uneducated, poverty-stricken grocery clerk to study some law books he found in the bottom of a barrel of household junk that he purchased for fifty cents. You have probably heard of him. His name was Abraham Lincoln. It is this desire that makes you want to wear the latest styles, drive the latest cars, and quote your brilliant children. It is this desire that lures many boys and girls into joining gangs and engaging in criminal activities. If you tell me how you get your feeling of importance, I'll tell you what you are. It sizes you up and determines your character. It is the most significant thing about you. For example, John D. Rockefeller got his feeling of importance by giving money to erect a modern hospital in Peking, China, to care for millions of poor people whom he had never seen and never would see. Dillinger got his feeling of importance by being a bandit, a bank robber, and a killer.

15-Second Timings

1. jhj jhj his his huh huh had had hit hit him him hat hat

2. ham ham heh heh hop hop hax hax hiz hiz hal hal har har

3. hay hay the the ash ash ugh ugh hug hug hag hag how how

4. huge huge high high hash hash heal heal half half hitch

5. hearth hearth height height highest highest hoggish hog

6. eighth eighth hunched hunched thought thought hardships

30-Second Timings

7. harsh harsh health health highly highly cheetah cheetah

8. harsher harsher hotshot hotshot highway highway hatchet

9. hunched hunched hitchhiker hitchhiker fishhook fishhook

10. That hitchhiker had a healthy habit of eating hot fish.

11. Hank held a hatchet and hammer ready to hack at boards.

12. The white whale jumped highest to reach the huge hoops.

1-Minute Timings

13. Hammer the shutters tightly to withstand the hurricane.

14. The Heathens are a hardy hiking group that hikes a lot.

14.   If you want to know how to make people shun you and
laugh at you behind your back and even despise you,
here is the recipe: Never listen to anyone for long and
talk incessantly about yourself. If you have an idea
while the other person is talking, don't wait for him
or her to finish. Just zoom right in and interrupt in
the middle of a sentence.

To be a good conversationalist, be an attentive
listener. To be interesting, be interested. Ask
questions that the other persons will enjoy answering.
Encourage them to talk about themselves and their
accomplishments. Remember that the people you are
talking to are a hundred times more interested in
themselves and their wants and problems than they are
in you and your problems. A person's toothache means
more to that person than forty earthquakes in Africa.
Think of that the next time you start a conversation.

PRACTICE WORDS FOR PARAGRAPH TIMING

accomplish accomplish appreciated appreciated grocery

uneducated uneducated poverty-stricken poverty-stricken

engaging engaging criminal criminal activities erect

character character determines determines Dillinger

Use the drill screen to practice the words below.

PRACTICE WORDS FOR PARAGRAPH TIMING

---

quibbling quibbling unhappy unhappy naturally naturally
quite quite zestfully zestfully obliged obliged extreme
reminder reminder thankful thankful different different

If you finshed the paragraph before the time is up, double-space and begin again. Keep typing!

1-Minute Timing   **All Letters Used, S.I.—1.3**

15.   A very long time ago a quibbling and quite
unhappy horse asked the gods for longer, thinner
legs, a neck like a swan, and a saddle that would
just grow naturally on its back. The gods zestfully
obliged and granted its wish. Much to its extreme
horror, the horse found that it had been changed
into an ugly camel. The gods told the camel that
they granted the wish as a reminder that it is
better to improve what you have and be thankful for
what you are.

15-Second Timings

1. buy buy yap yap day day yak yak yet yet yum yum lay lay

2. bye bye buy buy shy shy may may hay hay say say dye dye

3. your your ugly ugly yolk yolk easy easy yard yard layer

4. hobby hobby style style yellow yellow entry entry candy

5. travel travel yearly yearly gypsy gypsy young young yes

6. yummy yummy yardage yardage yonder yonder heyday heyday

7. Yvonne is a young cyclist with yearnings for skydiving.

30-Second Timings

8. today today dryly dryly verify verify yucca yucca byway

9. symptom symptom geology geology bicycle bicycle dynamic

10. loyalty loyalty keyboard keyboard entirely entirely bay

11. Yesterday Candey dreamed of a yellow nylon/vinyl dress.

12. That cyclist will buy a motorcycle or bicycle sometime.

13. Lylian has always enjoyed the dynamic hobby of geology.

PRACTICE WORDS FOR PARAGRAPH TIMING

incessantly incessantly interrupt interrupt zoom zoom

conversationalist conversationalist attentive attentive

Encourage Encourage accomplishments accomplishments

person's person's toothache toothache earthquakes earth

15-Second Timings

1. ire ire air air ide ide ice ice ill ill inn inn ink ink

2. kid kid tie tie fib fib dig dig bit bit gin gin lid lid

3. fig fig rib rib sir sir big big mit mit tin tin tid tid

4. mini mini ibis ibis city city quiz quiz kiwi kiwi icily

5. isn't isn't chili chili icicle icicle infirm infirm wit

6. livid livid militia militia civilians civilians ability

30-Second Timings

7. ignites ignites insists insists initial initial insipid

8. incline incline silicon silicon inflict inflict illness

9. abilities abilities inclined inclined inhibits inhibits

10. I imagine that Kim had an alibi the night of the crime.

11. Excited civilians insist that the military inhibit war.

12. Chili was divided into thirteen categories for judging.

1-Minute Timings

13. Last night thieves seized some silicon chips from here.

14. The county by the river isn't immune to morning crimes.

15.   A jovial Russian woman lived with her husband and
    four children in a very small house. When her husband's
    parents lost their home, she had to take them in. The
    coughing of the old folks and the crowding was
    unbearable. In exasperation, she went to the village
    wise man who was known for helping many people solve
    their problems. She asked what she should do; she was
    afraid she was going crazy. He asked her to bring her
    cow into the house and come back and see him next week.
    She came back and reported that life was as unbearable
    as ever. This time he asked her to also bring her
    chickens into the house. A week later she returned and
    reported that her house was a mess of chicken feathers,
    cow dung, and people. She couldn't stand it. The wise
    man told her to now take out the chickens. The next
    week she reported that without the chickens it was
    definitely better, but it was still an absolutely
    miserable situation. The wise man told her to take out
    the cow and that would solve her situation. She did.
    Without the chickens and cow to contend with, the
    woman, her husband, the four children, and his two
    parents got along ever after quite peacefully. The
    moral? Everything is relative. Sometimes we don't know
    how well off we really are.

magic magic phrase phrase quit quit arguments arguments eliminate eliminate exceptional exceptional attentively amazing? amazing? probably probably person personality

Check Spacing:

Check the 'Setup' (see the 'Options' tab) for one or two spaces after a colon. A semi-colon is always followed by a one space.

1-Minute Timing   **All Letters Used, S.I.—1.4**

15.   Would you like to have a magic phrase that would quit arguments, eliminate ill feeling, create exceptional good will, and make the other person listen attentively? Sound amazing? This is the phrase: I don't blame you one bit for feeling as you do; if I were you I would probably feel just as you do. That phrase takes the wind out of any argument.

14.   Telling an employee that his or her performance is unsatisfactory is not a pleasant task. Most of us would dread doing it. Perhaps that is why we tend to avoid, postpone, or neglect this duty. However, this is one of the most important functions of management. How can a person perform better unless he or she is made aware of what they need to do to improve? On the other hand, if their work is judged to be of high quality, why should they maintain it at that level unless they know that their extra efforts are recognized and appreciated? As a manager, you have a responsibility to give everyone who works for you an honest, periodic appraisal of how they are doing. Seize every opportunity to give well-deserved praise. If someone deserves a high rating, give it.

PRACTICE WORDS FOR PARAGRAPH TIMING

jovial jovial husband's husband's coughing coughing

unbearable unbearable exasperation exasperation crazy

couldn't couldn't miserable miserable peacefully peace

15-Second Timings

1. jar jar jot jot jkj jkj jhj jhj jmj jmj jnj jnj jag jag

2. jab jab jam jam jet jet job job jaw jaw jib jib jut jut

3. joy joy jay jay jav jav joj joj jog jog jew jew jig jig

4. jabs jabs juju juju jerks jerks jump jump jerk jerk jon

5. jaded jaded jolly jolly jambs jambs jelly jelly jackets

6. joints joints juniors juniors jumping jumping judiciary

30-Second Timings

7. jewel jewel jiffy jiffy jaunt jaunt judge judge justice

8. jogged jogged jaunty jaunty adjourn adjourn jointly jag

9. jeopardy jeopardy jamboree jamboree juveniles juveniles

10. The objective of the jury in the judicial system is ok.

11. Jamming objects into the jam and jelly jars broke them.

12. John and Jack enjoyed jogging on their journey to Java.

1-Minute Timings

13. Jason's jealousy almost put his job in jeopardy Monday.

15-Second Timings

1. sxs sxs jax jax tax tax axe axe six six box box exe exe

2. ext ext exp exp pox pox oxe oxe tox tox fix fix mix mix

3. exam exam axle axle hoax hoax taxi taxi exit exit extra

4. toxin toxin index index excel excel sixty sixty pretext

5. expert expert oxygen oxygen reflex reflex excuse excuse

6. expressly expressly saxophone saxophone exhaust exhaust

7. The executive expressed extreme exhaustion at pressure.

30-Second Timings

8. boxer boxer relax relax export export mixer mixer expel

9. exhale exhale examine examine excise excise expects sax

10. excluded excluded mixtures mixtures executive executive

11. Taxi rides are a luxury; expect to pay excessive rates.

12. That exhibitor exhorted the boxer to exclude exercises.

13. Maxey will examine the exhaust and fix those vexations.

PRACTICE WORDS FOR PARAGRAPH TIMING

performance performance unsatisfactory unsatisfactory

postpone postpone recognized recognized periodic period

appreciated appreciated responsibility responsibility

well-deserved well-deserved management management extra

exactly exactly widely widely varying varying opposite
opinions opinions believe believe zippy zippy decisions
considers considers possible possible around around zip

1-Minute Timing   **All Letters Used, S.I.—1.4**

14.   Facts are quite tricky things. Two people can

    look at exactly the same set of facts and come out

    with widely varying or opposite opinions. People

    tend to believe what they want to believe. Some

    people make zippy decisions and then look around for

    some facts to back them up. A careful manager bases

    decisions on more than just facts--he or she

    considers the source and, if possible, checks a few

    of the facts out.

15.   If you want to excel in that difficult leadership
    role of changing the attitude or behavior of others,
    give the other person a fine reputation to live up to.
    When a fourth grade teacher in Brooklyn, New York,
    looked at her class roster the first day of school, her
    excitement and joy of starting a new term was tinged
    with anxiety. In her class this year she would have the
    school's most notorious bad boy. He caused serious
    discipline problems in the class, picked fights with
    the boys, teased the girls, and was fresh to the
    teacher. His only redeeming feature was his ability to
    learn quickly and whiz through school work easily. The
    teacher decided to face the problem student
    immediately. When she greeted her students the first
    day, she made little comments to each one of them. When
    she came to the problem student, she told him that she
    understood that he was a natural leader and she was
    going to depend on him to help make this class the best
    class in the fourth grade this year. She reinforced
    this over the first few days by complimenting him on
    everything he did and commenting on how this showed
    what a good student he was. With that reputation to
    live up to, even though he was only nine years old, he
    eagerly helped maintain classroom discipline all year.

quart quart raspberries raspberries zigzagged zigzagged
Strangely Strangely couldn't couldn't extra extra jar
co-worker co-worker behavior behavior something please

2-Minute Timing   **All Letters Used, S.I.—1.3**

15.   A small girl was asked by her mother to pick a
quart of raspberries. She didn't want to pick the
berries, so she zigzagged her way slowly with heavy
feet toward the raspberry patch. Then a happy
thought came to her. She would not pick just one
quart of raspberries; she would pick two quarts. She
would surprise her mother. Strangely, the thought
changed everything. She couldn't wait to see the
smile on her mother's face when she showed her the
extra quart jar. How do you show your pleasure when
a family member, friend, or co-worker does or says
something to please you? Do you give them a reason
to repeat the behavior?

14.   Some people think success is like a pie with only
so many slices to go around. Your success is not
measured by what others say or what others may
accomplish. All of us have a tendency to examine,
compare, and measure ourselves with others. But, the
truly happy people in this life know that it is not
against others that we compete. To paraphrase a quote
from the late Henry Fonda, he once said that a
thoroughbred racing horse never looks at the other
racehorses. It just concentrates on quickly running the
fastest race it can. On our track to success, we need
to fight the tendency to look at others and see how far
they have come. We tend to get discouraged and not give
ourselves credit for our successes. The only thing that
really counts is how we use our potential, that we run
our race to the best of our abilities, and that we
seize every opportunity to improve.

PRACTICE WORDS FOR PARAGRAPH TIMING

---

excel excel difficult difficult leadership leadership

reputation reputation excitement excitement anxiety

notorious notorious discipline discipline whiz whiz

immediately immediately beautifully beautifully depend

FOR PRACTICE:

Read and circle all errors in the paragraph below. Errors include transposing and other misspellings and spacing. You should find 17 errors.

A good salesperson is competative. He or she is is always competing, not only against others but against himself--triing to better his previous performence. Why is this a smart thing for peeple in sales to do? Because someone who is triing to reach a definite goal will make that extre bit of effort in in order to do it. A person with no definate gaol in mind doesn't have the same insentive. Break big gaols into little ones that can be achieved step by step. Do you want to open 100 new acounts this year? That's about two two new acounts per week, eight or nine new acounts per month.

FOR REAL:

Find a circle all spelling and spacing errors below. Select 'Proof Reading 2' from the 'Proof Readings' menu. Type the paragraph. It will word wrap automatically to the next line as you type. Proofread carefully—there is a 10 point error penalty for every error. Only the first attempt will record.

Keep your goals practicle. Aim high enought to strech yourself, but not so high you lose hope and give up after a week or two. Goals that are dificult, but not impossible, to atttain will help you keep yourself on the ball. Salespeople who keep records and and sit goals for themselves will sometimes find that thier performance isn't as good as it it ought to be. That's one of the best reasons for keeping score. It helps salespeople face the facts imediately; it keeps them from kidding themselves.Saalespeople who don't study thier performance and set higher goals are letting themselves of too easy.

15-Second Timings

1. sws sws wet wet two two was was way way war war web web

2. wax wax wok wok pew pew law law ewe ewe new new low low

3. ware ware work work wage wage when when wilt wilt water

4. wagers wagers wagged wagged wired wired windows windows

5. swallow swallow welfare welfare waxwork waxwork awarded

6. wallflower wallflower wholewheat wholewheat windowsills

7. The swift cowhand will win the worldwide award Tuesday.

30-Second Timings

8. widow widow write write wallow wallow willow willow wow

9. lowdown lowdown newsman newsman wearily wearily warship

10. waterways waterways interviews interviews worthwhile we

11. The window washer was awarded twelve trips to the snow.

12. Who wired the wrench to the bow of the warship at work?

13. Warjack browsed with the newsmen at the wrecked wagons.

PRACTICE WORDS FOR PARAGRAPH TIMING

measured measured accomplish accomplish compare compare

tendency tendency examine examine ourselves ourselves

paraphrase paraphrase thoroughbred thoroughbred quickly

discouraged discouraged potential potential opportunity

15-Second Timings

1. kik kik kit kit kip kip kat kat kal kal kos kos kam kam

2. key key kin kin Kim Kim kna kna kla kla ket ket aky aky

3. kick kick knee knee kept kept knit knit kirk kirk khaki

4. knack knack kinfolk kinfolk knuckle knuckle kookie keel

5. koalas koalas kitchen kitchen keynote keynote skunks ok

6. skylark skylark kickback kickback knockout knockout kid

30-Second Timings

7. kayak kayak kinky kinky kettle kettle knows knows skunk

8. kicker kicker khakis khakis knuckle knuckle trekked tek

9. kinship kinship kinfolk kinfolk kickback kickback frock

10. Karl trekked home with his knapsack, kilts, and kayaks.

11. The knotty pine had leaky knots between the dry cracks.

12. The kinky kitten kicked the kettle and knocked it down.

1-Minute Timings

13. Kim, the keen kennel keeper, was the speaker last week.

15.   When you fear that the worst will happen, your own negative thoughts may help to bring it about. A salesman was driving on a lonely country road one dark and rainy night and had a flat tire. Upon opening his trunk, he found that his lug wrench was missing. He could barely see a light from a farmhouse up the road. He set out on foot through the driving rain to the farmhouse. Surely the farmer would have a lug wrench he could borrow, he thought. Of course, it was late at night. The farmer would probably be asleep. Maybe he wouldn't want to answer the door. He will probably be angry at being awakened in the middle of the night. The salesman, walking blindly in the dark, stumbled on. He was soaked to the skin. The thought about the farmer being angry for being woke up made the salesman piqued. The farmer was obviously selfish and being an old buzzard. The salesman finally reached the farmhouse and hammered loudly on the door. A light went on inside, a window opened above, and a voice asked who it was. The salesman yelled back, his face white with anger. "You know darn well who it is, you jerk. You can keep your stupid lug wrench. I wouldn't borrow it now if you had the last one on earth." And he angrily stomped back to his car.

usually usually receive receive friendly friendly jolly

consistently consistently invariably invariably extra

phrase--chickens phrase--chickens buzzards buzzards

1-Minute Timing   **All Letters Used, S.I.—1.4**

14.   What we give, we usually receive in return. If
we are friendly, we make friends easily. If we are
jolly or pleasant to others, they are more pleasant
to us. If we are consistently kind, we quite
invariably reap the extra harvest of kindness in
return. To coin an old but true phrase--chickens do
come home to roost. Will chickens or buzzards be
coming to roost at your house?

people--things people--things genuinely genuinely Duke

unselfishness unselfishness thoughtfulness thoughtful

sizeable sizeable language language birthdays birthdays

3-Minute Timing   **All Letters Used, S.I.—1.4**

14.   If you want to make friends easily, put yourself
out to do things for other people--things that require
time, energy, unselfishness, and thoughtfulness.
Become genuinely interested in other people. When the
Duke of Windsor was Prince of Wales, he was scheduled
to tour a sizeable amount of South America. Before he
started out on that tour, he spent about six months
studying Spanish so that he could make public talks in
the language of the country. The South Americans
enjoyed it and loved him for it. Another man made a
point of finding out the birthdays of all his friends.
The birthdays were written on a calendar. When the
birthday arrived, there was a special card or note
sent. What a hit it made. Frequently, he was the only
person who had remembered. Becoming genuinely
interested in other people is the first step in
applying a valuable human relations rule: Make other
people feel important.

Reverend Reverend Graham Graham arrived arrived gaze searching searching invited invited Baptist Baptist answered answered didn't didn't everyone everyone

2-Minute Timing   **All Letters Used, S.I.—1.3**

15.   The Reverend Billy Graham jokes of a time early in his career when he arrived in a small town to preach a sermon. Wanting to mail a letter, his searching gaze quickly fell upon a young boy. He asked the boy where the post office was. When the boy told him, Graham thanked him and invited him to come to the Baptist church the next evening to hear him tell everyone how to get to heaven. The boy answered that he didn't think he would be there because Graham didn't even know his way to the post office.

15-Second Timings

1. fvf fvf val val vie vie veo veo vuv vuv van van vet vet

2. vex vex vaj vaj eve eve erv erv vat vat evv evv vag vag

3. viva viva very very vast vast save save veto veto given

4. violin violin living living virus virus visit visit vim

5. evolves evolves evolved evolved visible visible swerved

6. revolved revolved vivacious vivacious excavate excavate

7. A savory flavor is elevated by serving crisp anchovies.

30-Second Timings

8. revive revive voyage voyage vexing vexing living living

9. adverse adverse valuable valuable elevate elevate visit

10. vulnerable vulnerable vagabonds vagabonds vetoed vetoed

11. The evil grape virus invaded the valuable old vineyard.

12. Elvis wore a silver velvet vest to the vocal rehearsal.

13. Vivian vowed to visit vaudeville as a vexing diversion.

15-Second Timings

1. lit lit let let tel tel til til lay lay lie lie lop lop

2. lag lag all all lad lad law law low low lug lug lid lid

3. loll loll lilt lilt fell fell lull lull slug slug shall

4. skill skill ladle ladle libel libel lapels lapels halls

5. recall recall limply limply liable liable levers levers

6. parallel parallel willfully willfully hillbilly locally

30-Second Timings

7. llama llama fellow fellow frills frills level level ale

8. legally legally literal literal liberal liberal recalls

9. willfully willfully hillbilly hillbilly volleyball ball

10. Lyn is legally liable for libelous statements she made.

11. Lorri is willing to play volleyball with loyal players.

12. Will Larry willfully fulfill his pact to the hillbilly?

1-Minute Timings

13. Melvin salvaged the twelve ladles for the little girls.

15.   Make enjoyment of your work and your life a high
priority, rather than money. That is not to say that
the desire to be rich is bad. Almost everyone would
enjoy being wealthy; the desire for the luxuries of
life is healthy and normal. Over and over again,
however, dozens upon dozens of studies have shown that
people who find satisfaction in their work are the ones
who perform best, receive the quickest promotions, and
wind up making the most money in the long run. Those
who make money their primary goal rarely achieve their
economic goals and often wind up chronically unhappy.

        If you are stuck in a job that you do not enjoy,
you are not likely to put enough effort into it to go
very far even if you are being paid well. Money is
simply not enough as a motivator. It is a proven fact
that maximum performance comes from maximum enjoyment.
If you make enjoyment of your work and your life a top
priority, you will do your best. The result will be
success, and money follows success just as naturally as
daylight follows dawn.

remember remember person's person's fuzzy fuzzy jot jot

especially especially acquaintance acquaintance recent

conversation conversation description description fix

1-Minute Timing   **All Letters Used, S.I.—1.4**

14.   How can you make yourself remember a person's

name, especially if they are a recent acquaintance?

Names need to be clearly heard to not be fuzzy in

your memory. If necessary, ask to hear it again. Ask

how it is spelled if it is unusual. Repeat the name

several times during a conversation to help fix it

in your mind. Later, you might jot it down with a

brief description of the person.

qualified qualified personnel personnel promoted expert

vacancy vacancy competent competent doesn't doesn't

successors successors subconscious subconscious malice

transferred transferred puzzling puzzling performance

2-Minute Timing   **All Letters Used, S.I.—1.5**

14.   According to one qualified personnel expert, the
person who is just promoted is the very worst person to
recommend someone to fill his vacancy. No matter how
competent and loyal the departing employees may be,
they simply cannot resist recommending successors whom
they feel will do less well at the job. It is a
subconscious thing with outgoing employees, and almost
always is done without malice. It seems that it doesn't
make any difference whether they have been promoted or
transferred at the same company, or even if they are
leaving the company. This should not be puzzling. They
simply can't bear the idea that their successors may
match or surpass their own performance.

PRACTICE WORDS FOR PARAGRAPH TIMING

enjoyment enjoyment priority priority luxuries luxuries

dozens dozens satisfaction satisfaction promotions dawn

quickest quickest economic economic chronically unhappy

motivator motivator maximum maximum daylight daylight

quickly quickly experiment experiment honestly honestly

obviously obviously azure azure justified justified

all-important all-important practiced practiced conduct

2-Minute Timing   **All Letters Used, S.I.—1.3**

15.   Do you know how to make people like you quickly?
Try a little experiment. Pick out someone you meet
and try to make that person like you. Obviously, to
do this, you must say something nice, and not about
yourself. Ask yourself what there is about that
person that you can honestly admire. Do you admire
their head of hair? Or their deep azure blue eyes?
Or their deep voice? We are talking here of honest
and justified appreciation, not cheap flattery.
Then tell them about what you have found to admire.
You will have practiced the one all-important law of
human conduct, and that is: Always make the other
person feel important.

15-Second Timings

1. juj juj jut jut use use our our due due put put urn urn

2. guy guy out out cut cut but but gnu gnu duo duo tub tub

3. luau luau urge urge upon upon user user ugly ugly guide

4. usury usury uncle uncle fruit fruit cough cough surplus

5. saucers saucers unglued unglued unlucky unlucky uranium

6. ukuleles ukuleles curriculum curriculum untruth untruth

7. It is unwise and unfair to quickly jump to conclusions.

30-Second Timings

8. sunup sunup about about unsure unsure unfix unfix uncle

9. quarter quarter nuzzled nuzzled cucumbers cucumbers ump

10. tumultuous tumultuous unscrupulous unscrupulous uncouth

11. Biscuits and fruit juices are also suitable for brunch.

12. A furry and fuzzy squirrel touched the nose of a puppy.

13. The guests were uncouth and unruly at that Spring luau.

15-Second Timings

1. jmj jmj met met mum mum map map met met mod mod mad mad

2. maw maw maz maz max max may may mew mew moe moe man man

3. mums mums mama mama maim maim mine mine mime mime modem

4. mommy mommy common common summer summer micro micro mit

5. memory memory summer summer macrame macrame memoirs mil

6. maximum maximum minimum minimum mermaid mermaid minimal

30-Second Timings

7. miner miner memos memos mimic mimic common common comma

8. mummy mummy humming humming hammock hammock summary sum

9. momentum momentum memorandum memorandum memento memento

10. May will memorize the memo in a minimum amount of time.

11. Mail her six mementos of the Little Mermaid in Denmark.

12. Macy said the majority of miners in Mazie had hammocks.

1-Minute Timings

13. Those hamsters munched many meals in an amusing manner.

DIRECTIONS:

This is an exercise in proofreading and in following directions. Type the following personal business letter in block style—all parts of the letter begin at the left margin. Make all the corrections as marked. Follow the spacing directions in parenthesis and italics very carefully. The typed lines will not end exactly as shown below. If you aren't sure of some of the proofreading marks, check previous pages. Proofread your typing carefully. There will be a penalty of 10 points for every error, spacing or spelling. **Only the first attempt will record on the Progress Report.**

Select Proof Reading #4 in the Proof Readings Menu. Beginning on line 1, press the Enter key twelve times before typing the first line of your return address. Paragraphs will word wrap automatically.

(press return key 12 times)

1469 N. Galveston
Chandler, AZ 85224
Current Date (after date, press enter/return key 4 times)

Mr. Thomas Torrence
Mesa Public Schools
151 N. Jay St.
Mesa, AZ 85213 (press enter/return key 2 times to double space)

Dear Mr. Torrence:

Thank you for offering to to be the keynote speaker at this year's national Business Education Convention. It will be held in Nashville, Tennessee, the home of country and western music. Be sure to come early enough to tour the city and see the sights.

I understand you will need an over head projector, a screen, and a quick carrousel slide projector. We have already lined these up for you.

By the way, you will have approximately forty-five people in attendance at your workship.

Sincerely yours, (press enter/return key 4 times to name)

James Alderman

JA/xx (Your boss prefers his initials in upper case letters, yours in lower case letters. Put your initials in place of the "xx".)

questions questions expedite expedite cooperation solve

considered considered technique technique zealous zeal

1-Minute Timing   **All Letters Used, S.I.—1.4**

14.   No one likes to take orders. You can get the
same things done without giving orders by asking the
right questions. How long would it take you to
complete this job? Is there anything we can do to
expedite this order? Have you considered this? Do
you think this would work? This technique invites
zealous cooperation instead of rebellion, and gives
people a feeling of importance in being able to help
solve problems.

15.   If you are interested in being successful on the
       job and at home with your family, you must learn to
       control your temper. Lots of people have. A volatile
       and quick temper is one of the most damaging management
       handicaps you can possibly have. When your temper is
       aroused, you are reacting with your glands and not your
       brain. An angry reaction is never a smart one. When you
       do something in anger, it is almost never the
       intelligent thing to do. You do it because it satisfies
       your irritation, not because it makes sense.

(Double space between all paragraphs.)

       What is it that makes most of us angry? Usually
       it's when someone has shown a lack of respect for us.
       The snazzy image we have of ourselves has been
       offended. So, conceited souls that we are, we get
       furious. Instead, we should simply relax and be
       curious. Is our image that important to us? Is anyone
       else's opinion really worth getting angry about? How
       ridiculous! Handling people skillfully demands self
       control. People who want to be good at managing others
       must first learn to control themselves.

argument argument jealous jealous can't can't expert

rattlesnakes rattlesnakes earthquakes earthquakes avoid

zealously zealously non compos mentis convinced against

2-Minute Timing   **All Letters Used, S.I.—1.3**

15.   There is only one way under high heaven to get
    the best of an argument and that is to avoid it.
    Avoid it as you would avoid jealous rattlesnakes and
    earthquakes. You can't win an argument. You can't
    because if you lose it, you lose it; and if you win
    it, you lose it. Why? Well, suppose you triumph over
    the other man and shoot his argument full of holes.
    Perhaps you zealously prove that he is non compos
    mentis and that you are an expert. Then what? You
    will feel fine. But what about him? You have made
    him feel inferior and you have hurt his pride. He
    will resent your triumph. And a man convinced
    against his will, is of the same opinion still.

guests guests impression impression hadn't hadn't quick

squandered squandered expression expression jewelry

"I like you. You make me happy." "I Like you."

simplest simplest quickest quickest one's one's realize

2-Minute Timing   **All Letters Used, S.I.—1.4**

14.   At an elite dinner party in New York, one of the guests was a woman who had inherited a lot of money and was eager to make a good impression on everyone. She had squandered a modest fortune on sables, diamonds and pearls. But she hadn't done anything whatever about her face. It radiated sourness and selfishness. She didn't realize what everyone knows: that the expression one wears on one's face is far more important than the clothes or jewelry one wears. Actions speak louder than words, and a smile says: "I like you. You make me happy." A smile is the simplest and quickest way to make a good first impression.

PRACTICE WORDS FOR PARAGRAPH TIMING

successful successful volatile volatile handicaps you

intelligent intelligent irritation irritation snazzy

conceited conceited else's else's ridiculous! ridiculous!

opinion opinion skillfully skillfully reacting reacting

15-Second Timings

1. jnj jnj jan jan not not non non nod nod nip nip nix nix

2. nil nil naz naz tan tan run run bin bin sun sun nay nay

3. nine nine neon neon noun noun nano nano noon noon nanny

4. nylon nylon annoys annoys inane inane funny funny onion

5. cannon cannon cannot cannot dinner dinner channel penny

6. nunnery nunnery scanner scanner nonentity nonentity zen

30-Second Timings

7. ninth ninth ninny ninny penny penny nerves nerves linen

8. banned banned annoyed annoyed channels channels running

9. frenzied frenzied napping napping conference conference

10. A day nurse insisted that the ransom note go unnoticed.

11. That nanny asked the new teacher to censor these nouns.

12. A crazy convict hid new money in a landfill in Norwich.

13. The frenzied inventor encountered an annoying obstacle.

15-Second Timings

1. ftf ftf tat tat tuf tuf tax tax tot tot tan tan tar tar

2. tap tap tab tab yet yet bat bat tie tie vet vet wet wet

3. time time thin thin teen teen tell tell jets jets tests

4. tutors tutors attract attract twist twist statue statue

5. tablets tablets tourists tourists textile textile train

6. traumatic traumatic thermostat thermostat tattle tattle

30-Second Timings

7. tried tried trade trade study study jests jests tactful

8. typical typical quitter quitter typists typists toaster

9. intermittent intermittent strutting strutting technique

10. Tim writes creative articles that got noticed by Trent.

11. The toiling tutor tried to trim the study time of Troy.

12. The wretched cattle are too thin to sell at the market.

13. Teri is a typical typist, but Tam has better technique.

conversationalist conversationalist listener listener

Dazzle Dazzle acquaintances acquaintances rapt rapt

Exclusive Exclusive Reader's Digest quiet audience want

1-Minute Timing   S.I.—1.3

14.   An easy way to become a good conversationalist is to be a good listener and enjoy it. Dazzle your acquaintances with rapt attention. Exclusive attention to the person who is speaking to you is very important. It is very flattering to feel that what you have to say is important enough to hold another person's rapt attention. As the Reader's Digest once put it: Many persons call a doctor when all they want is a quiet audience.

15.   Professor Harry A. Overstreet said that action
springs out of what we fundamentally desire, and the
best piece of advice which can be given to would-be
persuaders, whether in business, in the home, in the
school, in politics, is: First, arouse in the other
person an eager want. He who can do this has the whole
world with him. He who cannot walks a lonely way.

(Double space between all paragraphs.)

        Jim was a little child who was underweight and
refused to eat properly. His parents used the usual
method of scolding and nagging, and with the usual
results. The parents decided to try to find out what
the boy really wanted. There was a bully on the street
where he lived that would always pull him off his
tricycle and ride it himself. Jim would come screaming
in a tizzy to his mother; the mother would make the
bully give back the tricycle. The parents decided to
try to use what the boy wanted. They told him that if
he would eat the things his mother put on his plate, he
would grow big and strong and that bully would be
afraid to pull him off his tricycle. As you can guess,
that quickly solved the eating problem. The parents
aroused an eager want in their boy, and the desired
action followed naturally.

extra extra strewn strewn antagonize antagonize quality

excellent excellent debris debris didn't didn't human

principles principles day's day's approval approval

3-Minute Timing   All Letters Used, S.I.—1.3

15.   A lady was having an extra room built onto her
house. For the first few days of the job she noticed
that the yard was strewn with the cut ends of
lumber. She didn't want to antagonize the builders
because they did excellent, quality work. So, after
the workers had gone home, she and her children
picked up and neatly piled all the lumber debris in
a corner. The following morning she called the
foreman to one side and told him how pleased she was
with the way the front lawn was left the night
before; it was nice and didn't offend the neighbors.
From that day forward, the workers picked up and
piled the debris to one side, and the foreman came
in each day seeking approval of the condition the
lawn was left in after the day's work. What human
relations principles did she practice?

PRACTICE WORDS FOR PARAGRAPH TIMING

complaints complaints zoom zoom interrupt interrupt

don't don't dangerous dangerous won't won't attention

expression expression patiently patiently Encourage

2-Minute Timing   **All Letters Used, S.I.—1.4**

14.   The safety valve in handling irate complaints is to
let the other person talk about the problem until the
emotion is gone. Just listen. Ask them questions. Let
them tell you a few things. If you disagree with them,
you may be tempted to zoom right in and interrupt. But
don't. It is dangerous. They won't pay attention to you
while they still have a lot of ideas of their own
crying for expression. So, listen patiently and with an
open mind. Be sincere about it. Encourage them to
express their ideas fully and tell their side several
times. When the angry emotion is gone, then you can
reason together.

PRACTICE WORDS FOR PARAGRAPH TIMING

Professor Professor fundamentally fundamentally desire

would-be would-be underweight underweight tizzy tizzy

screaming screaming persuaders persuaders tricycle

15-Second Timings

1. lol lol lot lot owl owl lul lul olo olo out out own own

2. oil oil oat oat oar oar ole ole oak oak one one odd odd

3. ooze ooze only only cool cool roof roof door door roomy

4. crooks crooks polio polio proof proof floor floor odors

5. oodles oodles cocoon cocoon oblong oblong cookout cooks

6. textbooks textbooks schoolroom schoolroom zoology ovens

30-Second Timings

7. onions onions option option voodoo voodoo floors floors

8. snoopy snoopy offshoot offshoot outlook outlook robotic

9. rooftop rooftop footstool footstool workbooks workbooks

10. The bulls prowled all over the potato and onion fields.

11. A snoopy shopper dropped the oblong stool on the floor.

12. A quick hawk hovered near a hole with thoughts of food.

13. The boys chose boring quotes from a book of poor prose.

15-Second Timings

1. sas sas sag sag sod sod sea sea see see ash ash shy shy

2. ask ask sat sat sit sit sam sam she she gas gas sez sez

3. same same sees sees skis skis star star slip slip smoke

4. bossy bossy stand stand snips snips asset asset success

5. wasn't wasn't masses masses hostess hostess assist says

6. obsessive obsessive scissors scissors suspects suspects

30-Second Timings

7. disks disks swiss swiss stress stress scene scene sours

8. massacre massacre address address shrink shrink swooped

9. obsesses obsesses assassins assassins smallpox smallpox

10. Jackson tasted squab mixed with seasonings at the mall.

11. Zebras seem stressed out at the zoo and didn't respond.

12. Sassing your sisters does not make a good relationship.

13. The boss says the system must address the assets sales.

quickly quickly extra extra appreciation appreciation

opinionated opinionated sizzling sizzling arguments

1-Minute Timing   **All Letters Used, S.I.—1.5**

14.   The sun can make you take off your coat more
quickly than the wind; and kindness, the friendly
approach with extra appreciation, can make very
opinionated people change their minds more readily
than all the jabs, bluster, storming, and sizzling
arguments in the world. Abraham Lincoln taught that
a drop of honey catches more flies than a gallon of
gall.

15.   Remember that a person's name is to that person the
sweetest and most important sound in any language. The
policy of remembering and honoring the names of his
friends and business associates was one of the secrets
of Andrew Carnegie's amazing leadership. He was called
the Steel King; yet he says himself that he was no
expert in steel and knew little about its manufacture.
He had hundreds of people working for him who knew far
more about steel than he did. But he knew how to handle
people, and that is what made him rich. Early in life,
he showed a flair for organization, a genius for
leadership. By the time he was ten, he had discovered
the importance people place on their own name. And he
used that discovery to win cooperation. To illustrate:
When he was a young boy back in Scotland, he obtained a
mother rabbit. Within a very short time, he soon had
many little rabbits. He was in a quandary because he
had nothing to feed them. But he had a brilliant idea.
He told the boys and girls in the neighborhood that if
they would go out and pull enough clover and dandelions
to feed the rabbits, he would name the bunnies in their
honor. The plan worked like magic, and Carnegie never
forgot it.

sporting sporting introductory introductory approached

wasn't wasn't yesterday yesterday receptive receptive

somewhere somewhere journey journey lifetime lifetime

3-Minute Timing   **All Letters Used, S.I.—1.3**

15.   A sporting goods store hired a golf pro to give
      from six to a dozen introductory lessons to new
      customers. One day two women approached him. He
      asked them if they would like to learn how to play
      golf. One replied that she wasn't interested
      because she learned how yesterday, but she had
      brought her friend to learn today. Very few things
      in this life are learned in a day, certainly not the
      art of managing people. It is a lifetime job. An
      effective leader must keep on learning. He or she
      must keep an open mind and be receptive to new
      ideas. Most of us make a good start, but many seem
      to quit somewhere along the journey of life. Charles
      Gow wrote that the two great laws of life were
      growth and decay. When things quit growing, they
      begin to die. This is true of people, business, or
      nations.

Mark Twain honesty honesty extremely extremely zero

valuable valuable inevitably inevitably rejection truth

2-Minute Timing   **All Letters Used, S.I.—1.4**

14.   Mark Twain once said: When in doubt, tell the
truth. Perhaps we should all be in doubt more often.
Honesty is an extremely valuable tool in selling. There
will no doubt be occasions when it will seem that the
truth might hurt your chances of making a sale. Maybe
so. But a lie will quite likely zero your chances of
making any future sales. Lies lead almost inevitably to
customer distrust and rejection in the future. Over the
long run, the truth, and nothing but the truth, is good
business practice.

PRACTICE WORDS FOR PARAGRAPH TIMING

person's person's language language remembering names

associates associates Carnegie's Carnegie's magic magic

manufacture manufacture organization organization early

illustrate illustrate cooperation cooperation Scotland

quandary quandary dandelions dandelions neighborhood

COMMON PROOFREADER'S SYMBOLS:

∧	insert
⌒	close up, eliminate the space
#	add a space or a line
⌿	delete
⌒ (transpose)	transpose (exchange places)
≡	upper case (capital letter/s)
lc	lower case (small letter/s)
⊏	move to the left
⊐	move to the right
stet	let it stand (ignore marking)

DIRECTIONS:

Find and circle all spelling and spacing errors below. Select 'Proof Reading 3' from the 'Proof Readings' menu. Type each line, pressing Enter after each line. Proofread carefully—there is a 10 point error penalty for every error. Only the first attempt will record.

The antique vase, #32 at the auction, sold for $1569.35.

careful: confusing numbers in dollar amounts is not costly.

Am I pleased with your performance on the last evaluation.

My mother will except the certificate for me on wednesday.

do it today--then tommorrow's load will be 100%% less.

the crazy Taxi Driver charged me $3.25 extra just for fun.

15-Second Timings

1. frf frf far far jar jar err err rag rag ram ram tar tar

2. rob rob rat rat rub rub car car row row rad rad ear ear

3. rain rain rear rear pear pear ripe ripe port port radar

4. rumor rumor rerun rerun error error carry carry worrier

5. records records barrier barrier remarry remarry rancher

6. refrigerator refrigerator overruns overruns rearranging

30-Second Timings

7. rower rower carrier carrier merrier merrier rumor rumor

8. career career really really courses courses reports rip

9. terrariums terrariums frustrating frustrating reporters

10. The extra prize was awarded to Jake for acquiring land.

11. Any abrupt ruptures to the eardrum may require surgery.

12. Worry and hurry creates tensions, anger, and weariness.

13. Rose will race to restore order and report to ranchers.

15-Second Timings

1. p;p p;p pop pop pup pup peg peg pry pry pep pep pit pit

2. pod pod pry pry paz paz pax pax pen pen pie pie pet pet

3. pact pact prep prep prom prom play play jump jump pupil

4. quips quips poppy poppy Peter Peter ponds ponds snipped

5. poppies poppies peppers peppers support support prompts

6. peppermints peppermints puppeteers puppeteers pampering

30-Second Timings

7. papal papal popped popped zipper zipper perplex perplex

8. paprika paprika plopped plopped pompous pompous perhaps

9. presupposes presupposes prosperous prosperous publicize

10. Peter spoke with poise on the pompous plywood platform.

11. Push the pumps upward to stop the pond of putrid water.

12. The places for pleasant picnics had nicely paved paths.

13. The popular puppeteers used a purple puppet for a prop.

bouquets bouquets compliment compliment extreme extreme

syrup syrup encouragement encouragement jumping over

corporate corporate self-defeating self-defeating think

recognize recognize recognition recognition respect

3-Minute Timing   **All Letters Used, S.I.—1.4**

15.　　　Some managers have trouble passing out bouquets. They pay a compliment about as often as they get a tooth pulled. A few go to the other extreme and pour syrup all over people. Neither is effective. Some managers refuse to give praise for good ideas or a job well done simply because they are jealous. If you give a worker a lot of praise and encouragement, the next thing you know they are jumping over you on the corporate ladder. That's how they feel. Actually, that is self-defeating thinking. When you recognize good work, you give an employee the will to do better work. If you don't recognize it, you are feeding one of the biggest gripes employees have, which is the lack of recognition. The best thing to do every time is to give credit where credit is due. You will be a better manager for it and you will win much more respect.

zealous zealous saleswoman saleswoman jujube jujube

cosmetic cosmetic prospects prospects complexion Always

sensitive sensitive intuition intuition approaches

1-Minute Timing   **All Letters Used, S.I.—1.5**

14.   A zealous, but kind, saleswoman found that she
sold more of a certain jujube cosmetic cream when
she stopped telling prospects that it would restore
their complexion. She began saying it would
preserve their complexion. Always be sensitive to
intuition and be quick to try new approaches.

paraphrase paraphrase Somerset Maugham exhibit exhibit

egotistical egotistical self-complacent self-complacent

Quite Quite jealous jealous bizarre bizarre behavior

1-Minute Timing   **All Letters Used, S.I.—1.7**

14.   To paraphrase writing from Somerset Maugham, the common idea that success spoils people by making them vain, egotistical, and self-complacent is very wrong. Quite to the contrary, they most often exhibit behavior that is humble, tolerant, and kind. Failure makes people jealous, cruel, and bitter, and can lead to bizarre behavior.

technique technique affection affection motives motives

ulterior ulterior swizzle swizzle genuinely genuinely

doesn't doesn't interested interested tomorrow tomorrow

3-Minute Timing   **All Letters Used, S.I.—1.3**

15.   Who has the greatest technique for winning friends?
You may meet him tomorrow coming down the street. When
you get within ten feet of him, he will begin to wag
his tail. If you stop and pat him, he will almost jump
out of his skin to show you how much he likes you. And
you know that behind this show of affection on his
part, there are no ulterior motives: he doesn't want to
sell you any real estate, and he doesn't want to marry
you. Did you ever stop to think that a dog is the only
animal that doesn't have to work for a living? A hen
has to lay eggs, a cow has to give milk, and a canary
has to sing. But a dog makes his living by giving you
nothing but love. The lesson you can learn from an
expert, a friendly dog, is that you can make more
friends in two months by becoming genuinely interested
in other people than you can in two years by trying to
swizzle other people into being interested in you.

15-Second Timings

1. aqa aqa qqa qqa que que qua qua qui qui quo quo qiq qiq

2. aqq aqq quu quu uqq uqq quq quq qia qia qub qub qoq qoq

3. quip quip quid quid quiz quiz quay quay quads quads qua

4. squab squab quick quick quake quake quarry quarry squaw

5. qualities qualities questions questions quickly quickly

6. questions questions quarterly quarterly quicksand quart

30-Second Timings

7. queen queen quest quest equals equals equip equip quits

8. queasy queasy square square quizzed quizzed quasars quo

9. acquired acquired squadron squadron requirement require

10. The axe required an adjustment to meet quality control.

11. Quenton quietly asked questions about the town squares.

12. The aquariums were examined for cracks from earthquake.

13. Quietly take the eleventh required quiz in the morning.